ENGAGE THE COLLEGE EXPERIENCE

How to excel in the classroom & Beyond

Claudia Lilie • Christine Vodicka

Kendall Hunt
publishing company

Cover image © Shutterstock, Inc.

Kendall Hunt
publishing company

www.kendallhunt.com
Send all inquiries to:
4050 Westmark Drive
Dubuque, IA 52004-1840

ISBN 978-1-4652-3047-8

Printed in the United States of America
10 9 8 7 6 5 4 3 2

THIS BOOK BELONGS TO:

Andrew Crosby

Table of Contents

© brushingupl, 2012. Used under license from Shutterstock, Inc.

How to Make the Most of This Book

Welcome to the most helpful book of the semester! This book has been designed to help college students succeed academically by including a variety of self-management tools. *Engage the College Experience* is loaded with tips, ideas, and guides to assist you from start to finish. There are a number of helpful templates that you may want to use over and over again. You may want to photocopy the guides and activity logs so you can implement the organizational strategies all semester long. Whether you are planning a visit to your advisor or prepping for a big project, we kept *your* needs in mind when designing this book.

Acknowledgements

Thank you to Erin Hanrahan and Andrea Clos, English SLA Leaders and CSU students, for their contributions and proofreading. Thank you to Stephanie Sredniawa and Halley Daniels, Success Coaches and CSU students, for the great examples and contributions. Thank you to Ann Marie Smeraldi, First Year Experience Librarian, for her continued support and contributions. We appreciate the contributions of material from Carrie Love and Brittany Goldowski, CSU graduate students. This book would not be possible without the continued support of Dr. Rosemary Sutton and Dr. Eric Yeager.

Lastly, Christine would like to thank Dr. Robin Wisniewski for introducing her to the world of study skills and college success. Claudia would like to thank the instructors of Introduction to University Life who inspire her to continually explore success strategies for students. You are what make CSU's incoming freshman students and the ASC 101 course successful.

CHAPTER ONE:

GO FOR IT!

Motivation and Goal Setting

"If you don't know where you are going, you'll end up someplace else." –*Yogi Berra*

College can be overwhelming. There is the newfound freedom, the new friends, the assignments that are all due at the same time, and the list goes on and on. By now you probably are realizing that college is not "High School Part Two." College is an experience all on its own!

There are several reasons for going to college. The majority of students enrolled are preparing themselves for a career. Some are returning to prepare for a career change. Then, there are some that do not really know why they are here. Perhaps they had pressure from family to attend or feel it is their only option. Whatever the reason you are here, *it is imperative to be clear about your goals*.

Perhaps you have heard of the famous acronym, **SMART**, for goal setting. Goals, whether large or small, should be **SPECIFIC, MEASURABLE, ATTAINABLE, REALISTIC, and TIMELY.**

Here are examples of **not** so smart goal setting:

KIMBERLY: ***"I want to lose 30 pounds in a month for my sister's wedding."***

NED: ***"I have to pass my Math 116 class."***

DAMON: ***"Maybe I should start on a portfolio or looking for a job."***

What is wrong with each one of the examples above?

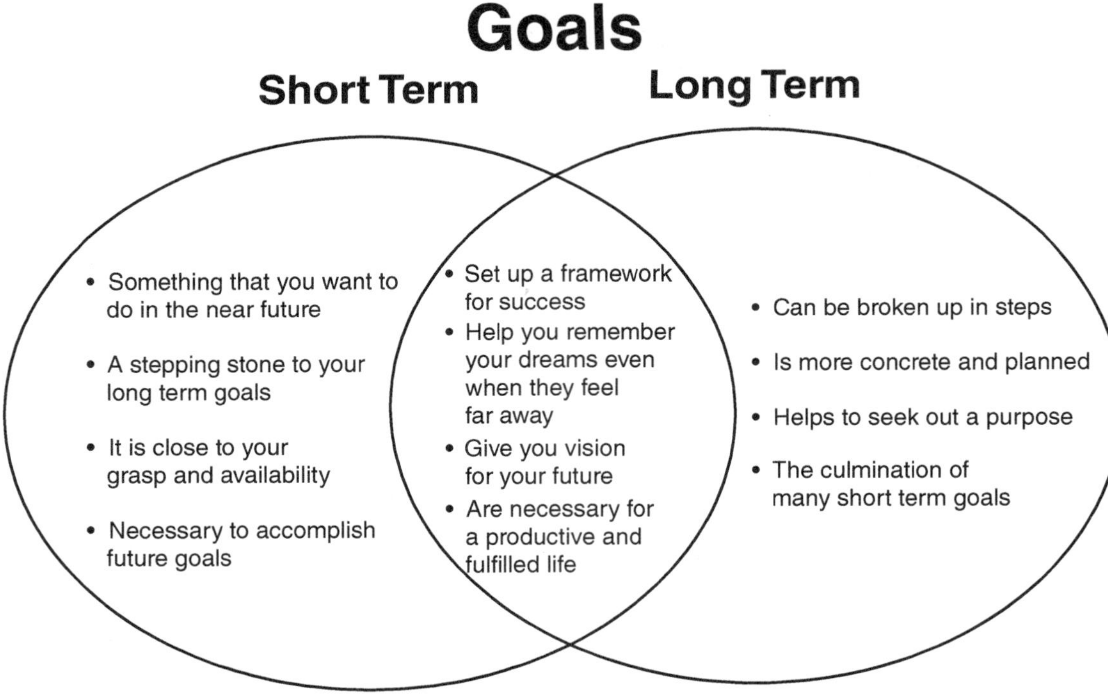

Fill in your own!

Kimberly's goal is not attainable! Who loses thirty pounds in a month? Even if the goal was attainable, she could strengthen her goal by adding a date. Here is her goal revised:

"I will lose two pounds per week by counting calories, keeping a food journal, and walking for thirty minutes five times per week. I will do this by Emily's wedding on June 24, 2013."

Whoa! What a difference! Now onto Ned's goal. Ned wants to pass his MTH 116 class. There is a lot of work to be done for this goal. Ned's goal is not specific, measurable, or timely. How would Ned's goal read if it were written using SMART goals?

Rewrite Ned's goal for a little practice:

Semester Goals

Now it's your turn! Following the example below, write three SMART goals for the semester.

Place a check in the correct category if the goal is:

SPECIFIC, MEASURABLE, ATTAINABLE, REALISTIC, and TIMELY.

Are Your Goals SMART?	S	M	A	R	T
Damon's Example: I will begin my job hunting portfolio by March 2013, and it will include letters of recommendation, transcripts, resume, and samples of my work.	✓	✓	✓	✓	✓
GOAL 1:					
GOAL 2:					
GOAL 3:					
GOAL 4:					

NOTE TO SELF: Write your goals on index cards and place them in places where you will see them (bedroom mirror, in your planner, on the refrigerator, etc.). Goals do no good if you write them and then forget about them!

Five Year Plan Treasure Map

Have you ever really thought about where you would like to be five years from now? Do you want to graduate by then? What steps do you need to take towards graduation? When would you like to start your job hunt? Do you want to relocate? What type of career do you desire? The questions are endless, but you can get a grip by completing this *Five Year Plan Treasure Map*! This map contains both short term and long term goals. Follow along the dotted line that you create to see how the ultimate goal is put into action by reaching the smaller ones first.

Directions:

1. Beginning with today's date, start at the X marked "you are here." Write the date and where you are in your plan (for instance, enrolled at CSU for 12 credits towards engineering degree: Spring 2012).
2. Next, visualize where you would like to be five years from now. This is your **long-term goal**. Write in your end goal, including the **specific details**. The more detailed you are the better! For instance, instead of "get a job as an engineer," one would write, "be hired as a civil engineer for the Ohio Environmental Protection Agency by June 2017."
3. Next, draw your path. Some people prefer a direct path from A to Z but others like to draw more of a zigzag line. See the example on the next page.
4. Along your path, add in smaller, **short-term goals**. When do you need to visit your advisor, look into internships, develop a resume, etc.? Be sure to keep with the SMART goals!
5. Sign and date your five year plan to make it official!
6. POST this map where you can see it on a daily basis.

Get Your Priorities Straight!

Don't get yourself flustered! It may seem there are an infinite amount of tasks you need to take care of and not enough time. Make it easy for yourself and break the tasks down. Write down when they are due according to the dates. You can do this on a monthly, weekly, or daily planner, but if that doesn't work for you, try using a priority sheet instead. The priority sheet is a month broken down into four parts: past due, due this week, due next week, and due this month. This is an easy way to organize everything you need to complete by documenting assignments, appointments, exam days, or even outside activities such as going to the gym.

© RetroClipArt, 2012. Used under license from Shutterstock, Inc.

A template has been included for you, in addition to a student example on pages 7–8.

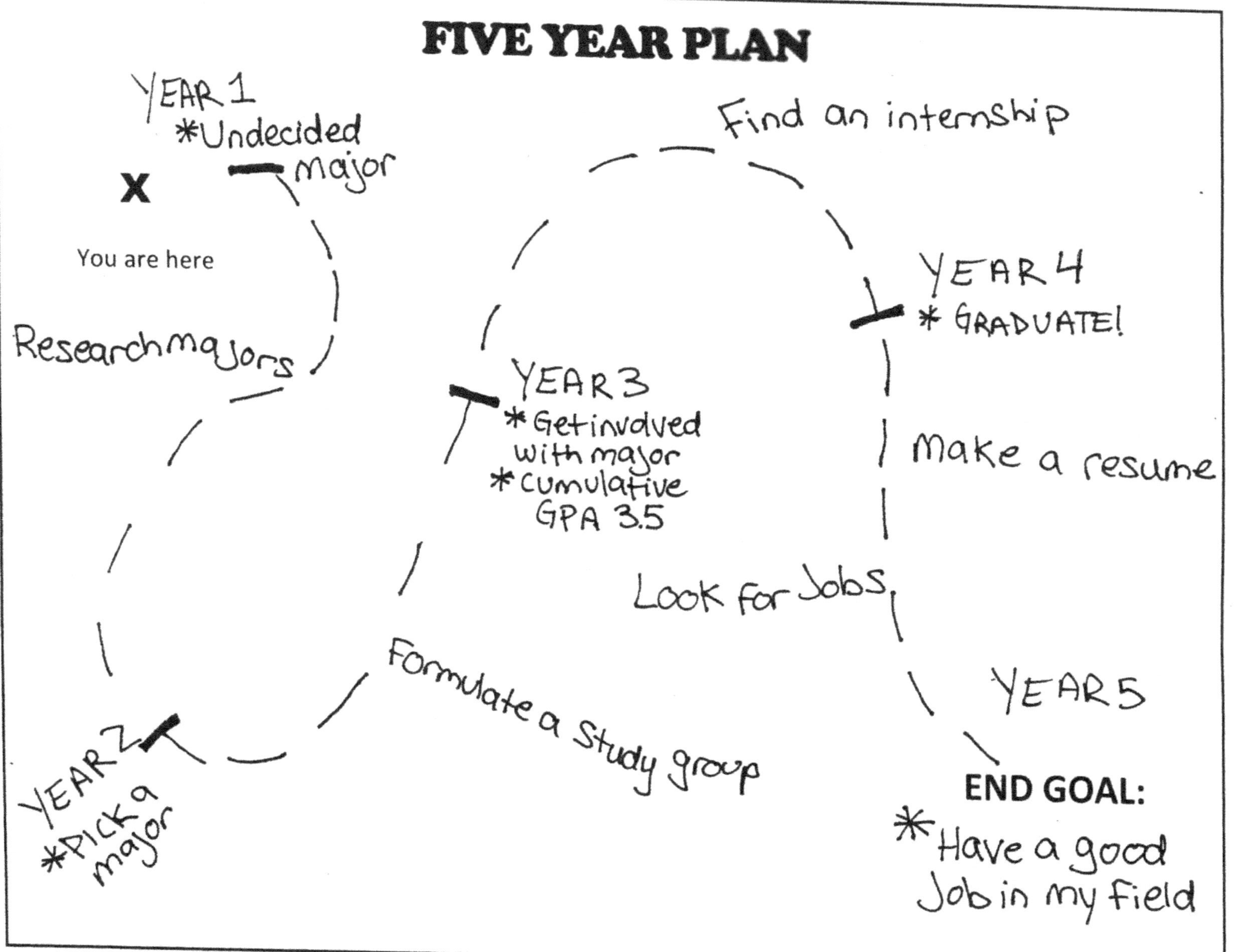
FIVE YEAR PLAN
YEAR 1
*Undecided major
X
You are here
Research majors
YEAR 2
*Pick a major
Formulate a study group
YEAR 3
*Get involved with major
*cumulative GPA 3.5
Look for Jobs
Find an internship
YEAR 4
*GRADUATE!
Make a resume
YEAR 5
END GOAL:
*Have a good Job in my field

FIVE YEAR PLAN

X

You are here

END GOAL:

PRIORITIES

Week of: SEPTEMBER 11th

DUE TOMORROW or PAST DUE

TO DO	DUE BY
1. Finish BIO 201 lab	9/11
2.	
3.	
4.	
5.	

DUE THIS WEEK

TO DO	DUE BY
1. ASC presentation	9/14
2. MTH 116 Chapter 3	9/15
3. Talk to BIO professor	
4.	
5.	

DUE NEXT WEEK

TO DO	DUE BY
1. BIO 201 Lab	9/18
2. Online BIO 200 Quiz	9/19
3.	
4.	
5.	

DUE THIS MONTH

TO DO	DUE BY
1. ENG 100 essay	9/28
2. Go to gym 2x a week	
3.	
4.	
5.	

PRIORITIES Week of: ____________________

DUE TOMORROW or PAST DUE

TO DO	DUE BY
1. ____________	______
2. ____________	______
3. ____________	______
4. ____________	______
5. ____________	______

DUE THIS WEEK

TO DO	DUE BY
1. ____________	______
2. ____________	______
3. ____________	______
4. ____________	______
5. ____________	______

DUE NEXT WEEK

TO DO	DUE BY
1. ____________	______
2. ____________	______
3. ____________	______
4. ____________	______
5. ____________	______

DUE THIS MONTH

TO DO	DUE BY
1. ____________	______
2. ____________	______
3. ____________	______
4. ____________	______
5. ____________	______

Discussion: Goal Setting and Motivation

When I came to college I thought I wanted to be a teacher. After two years I changed my major to psychology. Then I learned that I needed to attend graduate school in order to get a job in the psychology field. I am having a hard time deciding what to do. Money is an issue and I am almost at my student loan limit.

– Tonya

I feel like I will never graduate. When I started college I had one major goal . . . to graduate. That is it, plain and simple. What am I doing wrong and how do I stay motivated while on the "five-year college plan"?

– Josh

My advisor once told me about S.M.A.R.T. goals and I never really tried setting them. I thought it was just another lame acronym. Now that I am on academic probation with a 1.5 GPA, what are some examples of smart goals I could apply?

– June

CHAPTER TWO:

Make Time to Make Time

Time Management

"The key is in not spending time, but in investing it." –*Stephen R. Covey*

There are several obstacles when it comes to time management. Many college students have to learn to balance a full course load with work and/or family. Even students that live at home and don't work can struggle with time management. Why? Not scheduling study time!

Who hasn't pulled an all-nighter or waited until the very last minute to start on a project? Life happens, but you need to have a plan. When friends suggest that you pay a visit to the local Starbucks, be sure that you get your studying, reading, and homework done first. You will want to convince yourself that you will get your work done in the evening once you get home. But who wants to read about the laws of physics and solve equations late at night after the basketball game or concert?

When entering college, you may not realize the little things you need on your way to success. One thing that is commonly overlooked by students is a datebook or calendar. Tracking your life is important when in college. You will have many due dates for various assignments, work, or other outside activities you're involved in. Don't let all of that overwhelm you. When you have a thousand things running through your brain, it's easy to forget things if you haven't written them down. So, PUT IT ON PAPER! Once you have written everything you need to do on a calendar . . .

1. You **will be less stressed** now that you have written everything down and can physically see what it is you need to accomplish.
2. **You have more time** to finish a future project or study for exams.

3. You have less to do than you think. Since your brain is a little scattered you might be overthinking. You're most likely assuming you have more work to do than what is actually in front of you.

Follow These Rules and Rule School!

Rule #1: Avoid procrastinating at all costs. Just because nothing may be due this week or next week does not mean it's time for a two week party. Starting on projects well before they are due gives you more time to perfect the final product. This leads to better grades.

Rule #2: Break larger goals into smaller ones. Wait, this is not the goal setting chapter! Well, after you break down the large goals, do some *backwards planning*. Work backwards and schedule the goals into your planner.

Rule #3: Use a schedule! Whether you use a day planner, the templates in this book, or your phone, set a schedule! Determine where your open hours are and schedule study sessions within this time. Use an alarm/timer on your phone to keep you focused and on track.

Rule #4: Take advantage of any "found time." The time spent waiting for the bus, standing in line for the new Xbox game, or waiting in the doctor's office can all add up! Use a study log to track your study time and better understand your habits.

© RetroClipArt, 2012. Used under license from Shutterstock, Inc.

168 Hours

Did you know that there are 168 hours in one week? The 168 hours tracker on the next page allows you to see how you REALLY spend your time. Perhaps you think you study every night for hours, but it is actually just 30 minutes per night. Ouch.

Starting with tomorrow morning, begin to track when you wake up, when you are in class, when you commute, when you shop, when you go online, when you study, etc. You may be surprised at the patterns you see at the end of one week.

Take this activity a step further by highlighting different activities with different color highlighters. For instance, you can highlight all of your work time in green, all of your study time in yellow, class time in orange, and so on. This will help you get a better idea of how you spend your time as well as identify any time wasters that you should cut down on.

Once you have determined the time wasters and available time slots you were not using wisely, implement some new time management strategies, such as creating a study schedule. In a few weeks or months, track your 168 hours once more. Compare the life changes and experience the benefits of knowing where all of your time goes.

168 Hours: Activity Log

Name ______________________ Week of ______________________

	Sunday	Monday	Tuesday	Wednes	Thursday	Friday	Saturday
5:00am							
6:00am							
7:00am							
8:00am							
9:00am							
10:00am							
11:00am							
12:00pm							
1:00pm							
2:00pm							

Directions: On the day you receive the time log, start tracking how you spend your time every day, hour by hour. Do this for one full week. What did you learn about yourself?

168 Hours: Activity Log

3:00pm							
4:00pm							
5:00pm							
6:00pm							
7:00pm							
8:00pm							
9:00pm							
10:00pm							
11:00pm							
12:00am							

Directions: On the day you receive the time log, start tracking how you spend your time every day, hour by hour. Do this for one full week. What did you learn about yourself?

Daily Prioritizer

Date: September 7th

	Time	Activity
Urgent	7:00 - 8:00am	
* Advising Appointment	8:00 - 9:00am	BIO 200
	9:00 - 10:00am	↓
	10:00 - 11:00am	ASC 101
Important	11:00 - 12:00pm	↓
* Finish MTH 116 H.W.	12:00 - 1:00pm	Finish MTH 116 Homework
* Type BIO 201 lab	1:00 - 2:00pm	ENG 100
	2:00 - 3:00pm	↓
Ongoing	3:00 - 4:00pm	Advising Appointment
	4:00 - 5:00pm	
	5:00 - 6:00pm	WORK
	6:00 - 7:00pm	↓
Trivial	7:00 - 8:00pm	
* Lunch with Friends	8:00 - 9:00pm	Get off early
	9:00 - 10:00pm	
	10:00 - 11:00pm	Type BIO 201 lab

Additional Notes/Reminders:

Leave for New York on Sat. morning.

Start Packing tonight!!

Daily Prioritizer

	Time	Activity
Urgent	7:00 - 8:00am	
	8:00 - 9:00am	
	9:00 - 10:00am	
	10:00 - 11:00am	
Important	11:00 - 12:00pm	
	12:00 - 1:00pm	
	1:00 - 2:00pm	
	2:00 - 3:00pm	
Ongoing	3:00 - 4:00pm	
	4:00 - 5:00pm	
	5:00 - 6:00pm	
	6:00 - 7:00pm	
Trivial	7:00 - 8:00pm	
	8:00 - 9:00pm	
	9:00 - 10:00pm	
	10:00 - 11:00pm	

Weekly Planner

Time	Monday	Tuesday	Wednesday	Thursday	Friday	Saturday	Sunday
7:00 - 8:00							
8:00 - 9:00		BIO 200		BIO 200		Leave for NY	
9:00 - 10:00	BIO 201		STUDY		BIO SI		
10:00- 11:00				ASC 101			
11:00- 12:00							
12:00 - 1:00	MTH 116		MTH 116		MTH 116		
1:00 - 2:00		ENG 100		ENG 100			
2:00 - 3:00	GYM				GYM		
3:00 - 4:00							
4:00 - 5:00	STUDY		STUDY				
5:00 - 6:00		WORK		WORK			
6:00 - 7:00							
7:00 - 8:00							
8:00 - 9:00							
9:00 - 10:00							
10:00- 11:00							

Urgent	Important	Ongoing
✱ BIO 201 Quiz EVERY MONDAY ✱ MTH 116 H.W. Due EVERY FRIDAY	✱ Family Reunion All Weekend in New York	✱ ENG 100 essay due at the end of September

Weekly Planner

Week of: ______________________

Time	Monday	Tuesday	Wednesday	Thursday	Friday	Saturday	Sunday
7:00 – 8:00							
8:00 – 9:00							
9:00 – 10:00							
10:00 – 11:00							
11:00 – 12:00							
12:00 – 1:00							
1:00 – 2:00							
2:00 – 3:00							
3:00 – 4:00							
4:00 – 5:00							
5:00 – 6:00							
6:00 – 7:00							
7:00 – 8:00							
8:00 – 9:00							
9:00 – 10:00							
10:00 – 11:00							

Urgent	Important	Ongoing

MONTH OF: SEPTEMBER

Sunday	Monday	Tuesday	Wednesday	Thursday	Friday	Saturday
					1 *MTH H.W. 1	2
3	4 BIO201	5	6	7 Advising Appointment 3pm	8 *MTH H.W. 2	9 FAMILY Reunion in New York
10	11 BIO201	12	13 MTH	14 *ASC Presentation	15 *MTH H.W.3	16
17	18 BIO201	19 BIO200	20	21 BIO200	22 *MTH H.W. 4	23
24	25 BIO201	26	27	28 *ENG Essay	29 *MTH H.W5	30 Enjoy TODAY

KEY: EXAM QUIZ DUE DATES

MONTH OF:____________________

Sunday	Monday	Tuesday	Wednesday	Thursday	Friday	Saturday

PROJECT PLANNER

Name of Project/Assignment: ______________________________

Course: ______________________________

Due Date: ____________________

Goal Grade: ___________

STEP ONE: Describe the assignment. How many pages, how many points, what is expected?

STEP TWO: Determine the tasks you need to compete for the assignment. Use this checklist as a guide.

- ○ Conduct research
- ○ Talk to the professor
- ○ Meet with a tutor
- ○ Read the material
- ○ Form study group
- ○ Write a draft
- ○ Write a revision
- ○ Write a final copy
- ○ Create study guide
- ○ Study
- ○ Other:________________

STEP THREE: Assign each task a due date to keep you on track.

Task	Date to complete by

Study Log

At the beginning of the semester, a professor usually informs you how many study hours you should spend for that specific class. If it isn't given to you in the syllabus, ask the professor and write it down. You have a busy schedule, so are you really putting in the proper amount of study time for each class? Many students think they are, but after they have documented their study hours, realize it's not nearly enough.

Use the study log to document your study hours. Write down the days, class, and how long you studied for each week. You can block out time frames when you have a big chunk of time you can put into studying as well. Remember to take breaks during times like those (refer to example) so you don't overwhelm yourself. At the end of the week, add up your hours and find out if you have been slacking or are right on schedule.

• AT YOUR SERVICE

STUDY LOG

Week of: September 18th

Date	Subject(s)	Start Time	End Time	Total Time
9/18	BIO 200/201	4 PM	6 PM	2 hrs
	MTH 116	7 PM	8 PM	1 hr
9/19	ENG 100 (read)	10 AM	11 AM	1 hr
	BIO 200	11 PM	1 AM	2 hrs
9/20	MTH 116	10 AM	11 AM	1 hr
	BIO 201	11 AM	12 AM	1 hr
	BIO 200	4 PM	9 PM	5 hrs
		* 30min Break every hour *		
9/22	ENG 100 (ESSAY)	5 PM	7 PM	2 hrs

Grand Total: 15 hrs

STUDY LOG

Week of: ______________________________

Date	Subject(s)	Start Time	End Time	Total Time

Grand Total: ___________

STUDY LOG

Week of: ______________________________

Date	Subject(s)	Start Time	End Time	Total Time

Grand Total: ___________

Discussion: Time Management

I am a wife and mother to a two-year-old son. I'm also taking care of my sick father. On top of that I work part-time. I've just returned to school to finish my Bachelors. How do I make "me" time to reduce the stress levels?

– Karen

My grandmother recently died and my parents announced they are splitting. I am so overwhelmed I have been falling behind on homework assignments and my test grades reflect it. Where can I get help managing the stress and making time for school in my hectic life?

– Daniel

Between working full time, classes, homework, and studying, I'm lucky if I get three hours of sleep a night. It's really starting to take its toll on my health. What can I do to make more time for sleep in my life?

– Jennifer

CHAPTER THREE:

Learn to Learn

Organization, Studying, and Note-Taking

"When reviewing your notes before an exam, the most important will be illegible."
–Murphy's Law

Get Organized!

Perhaps you went shopping for school supplies prior to the semester. What items did you buy? The reason we ask is that we recommend a "tool kit." Having the right materials on hand will make your studying experience more effective, and quite possibly more enjoyable.

In fact, by having a variety of supplies at your fingertips, you can take your learning to the next level. Here are some examples of going above and beyond in the name of success:

- Use write-on tabs to tab your textbook chapters for easy reference.
- Use sticky notes to add questions and summaries to the textbook chapters (especially if you are hesitant to write in your book).
- Use two different color pens as a coding system. For instance, use a blue or black pen to take notes in class and use a red pen to add textbook notes to your lecture notes.
- Keep a two inch binder for each of your classes. Invest in a three hole punch and some tab dividers. Label each of your sections with headings such as:
    - Syllabus, class notes, homework, tests/quizzes, study guides, maps, research, papers, etc.

Tool Kit Shopping List

In addition to textbooks, the following are recommended for success . . .

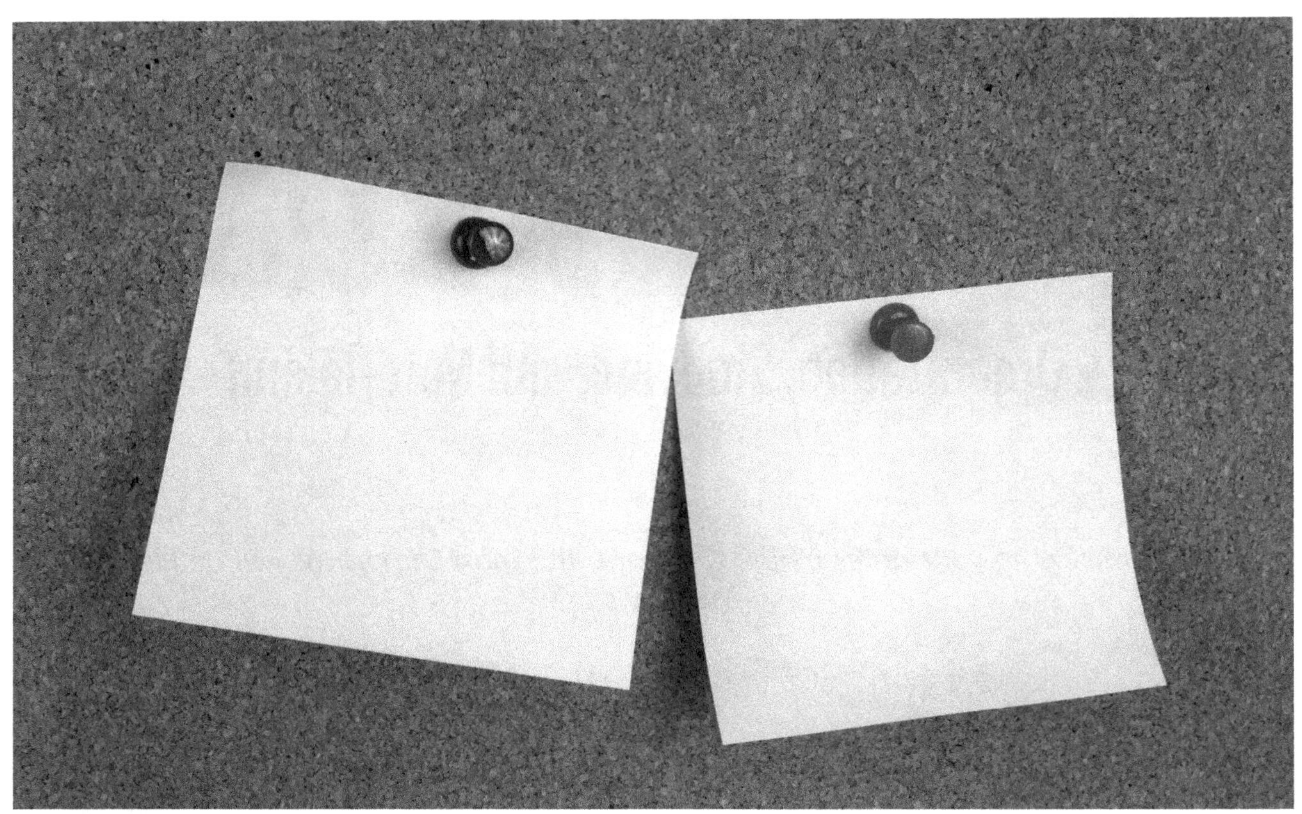

- ☐ 2" binder (one for each course)
- ☐ Three ring dividers with five tabs
- ☐ Three ring hole punch
- ☐ Ruled paper
- ☐ Paper in different colors (for mapping)
- ☐ Sticky notes
- ☐ 2 or more different color pens
- ☐ Highlighters
- ☐ Index cards (preferably various colors)
- ☐ Day planner*
- ☐ Calculator*
- ☐ Timer*

**These items are also available in the latest technology. Feel free to use your iPad or smartphone for these items. If you are too distracted by your technology, it is then recommended that you purchase the items separately as needed.*

So You Think You Can Study?

Before you sit down to study, ask yourself some quick questions first.

1. What environment do you study best in?

Where do you feel you will accomplish the most work?

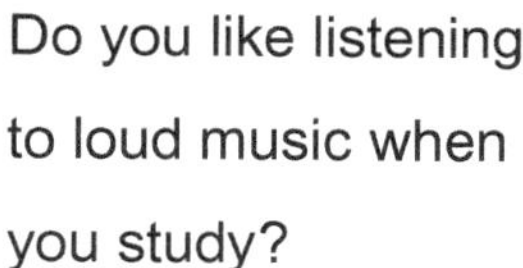

Do you like listening to loud music when you study?

Would you prefer going to a quiet coffee house?

Watching TV? Probably NOT a good spot, you'll end up watching the TV instead of studying.

All Images © RetroClipArt, 2012. Used under license from Shutterstock, Inc.

Is the sound level appropriate? Everyone likes different levels of background noise when they sit down to study. There are those who listen to music, go to coffee houses, or like a completely silent area. Whatever it is that you decide, remember, IT'S WHAT WORKS BEST FOR YOU! If you are finding that the study area you picked originally isn't working out because you're getting distracted, find a new location. It's never too late to try something new! Especially if the outcome of the change is beneficial to your study habits!

2. **Is it comfortable?** You want the area you're going to be in for a significant amount of time to be somewhere you feel comfortable, but not too comfortable. Don't kid yourself into thinking that lying in bed will be the perfect spot to start studying. Although it is comfortable, it's probably too comfortable. Chances are that you may fall asleep while trying to do your work.

3. **How's the lighting?** Make sure the lights are bright enough for you to see your books. If the lights are dim, you will find that you're squinting and straining your eyes, making you tired. So, find a well-lit spot. Something bright enough to keep you awake but not an area that is so bright it's blinding.

4. **Is the area uncluttered?** Make sure the area you picked is free of clutter. If you're sitting in a spot that has random items scattered around that are NOT associated with what you're studying, they will distract you. Let's be real here, you probably don't want to study so, if you have a bunch of random stuff in front of you, chances are you'll get distracted by it and won't study.

5. **Do you have all the supplies you will need?** Before you get curled up with your books, make sure you have everything you need before you get comfortable. You don't want to keep getting up to get pens, markers, etc., when you're ready to study. It will distract you and take away from study time.

Top 10 Study Tips

By: Halley Daniels, CSU Success Coach

10. Be sure to study in a quiet place where you are able to really focus and concentrate. Keep all of your study supplies (note cards, calculator, pens, paper, etc.) in the same place, so that when it comes time for you to study, you are not wasting time searching for these items.
9. Take some extra time to research or learn about new study techniques, like outlining, memory cards, concept maps, annotating. You may discover a new technique that helps you to retain information better than a previous method you had used. Also, go to the Tutoring and Academic Success Center (Main Classroom 233) to sign up with a tutor or a success coach, both of whom can help you immensely with either specific subjects or perfecting study skills.
8. Talk to your professors and become familiar with them. This will show your professors that you care about the class and your grade, and will help you out in the long run. Also, speak with your professors before tests to inquire what will be covered on exams, so that you know exactly what to study.
7. Make sure you take periodic breaks throughout your study time. Try to study for 50 minutes and then take a 10 minute break and repeat. When you take your break, try to empty your mind of studying and focus your attention elsewhere. A timer is also a great tool to use so that you do not keep glancing at the clock to know when your break is (there is probably a timer in your phone!). Also, you may want to go for a short walk or eat a snack, so you can come back to studying refreshed and ready to focus again.
6. As you study, highlight or put a star next to topics that you do not know as well as others, so that you remember to study those topics harder. This will allow you to spend more time on topics you aren't as familiar with, rather than spending equal amounts of time on all topics.

5. While you are studying, be sure to minimize distractions like the Internet, texting, talking on the phone, etc. so that you can really focus and concentrate on the material.
4. Get a study buddy from your class! A study buddy is a great person to study with because they learn the same material that you do. This can also help studying to be livelier and more engaging, which in turn could help you retain the information better.
3. Be sure to review the previous lecture's material a few minutes before your next lecture. If you do this regularly, you will be able to continuously form the connections of the topics you are learning from lecture to lecture. This will also help you be able to get a better handle on what you will be learning about during that day's lecture, so that you can understand the material better, as well as ask important questions.
2. Schedule yourself permanent study blocks or 'study halls' in your weekly schedule so that your study time does not accidentally get cut out. If you form this habit at the beginning of the semester, you will come to think of study time as an integral part of your schedule, rather than a chore. Also, having a permanent study block will ensure that you do study and not put it off.
1. Begin to study right after the test! After you take an exam, you may want to take a break from learning and studying. However, it is important to begin studying for the next exam right away so you do not lose touch from your school work, and also so you do not stop the flow of learning from topic to topic.

Learning to Learn Quick Tips

- Schedule, Schedule, Schedule!! Studying and learning involves time, and finding this time may be a challenge (especially when you are in college). Develop a time management plan by creating a weekly schedule of your classes, work schedule, and activities to help you see where you can fit in extra time devoted to learning content. Perhaps you have ten minutes waiting for the bus, 7 minutes waiting for your food to thaw, or 15 minutes waiting for your laundry to dry! These valuable times will add up and you will reap the benefits of your preparation!
- Know Yourself: Learn not only about your preferred mode of learning, but how you can incorporate your personal style and your learning. Are you a visual learner? You might want to think about using concept cards, drawing out ideas, or creating diagrams or visual organizers. Are you an auditory learner? Then you may want to 'think aloud' the important concepts in your classes with a study buddy and taking a practice test orally may be very reinforcing.
- Give me a break! That's right, give yourself the freedom to pause to give your hardworking mind a breather, rather than cramming tons of information.

Study Buddy Information Tracker

Why are Study Buddies important?

- Compare notes from class and improve your notes
- Quiz and learn from each other's strengths
- Study through discussion
- Create and share study guides
- See what you missed in class
- Increased motivation

Course	Student Name	Phone	Email	Best Days/Times

Guidelines for Studying with Peers / Study Groups:

1. Come prepared with textbook, notes, laptop (if needed), and questions!
2. Meet in a quiet, public place.
3. Choose your study buddies wisely!
4. Limit the number of study group members to 4 to 6.
5. Set an agenda and stay on track. A moderator or timekeeper helps.

Note-Taking 101

Just. Take. Notes. It's that simple. Do not rely on your memory to get you a good grade on the test. Oftentimes there will be weeks between tests. I don't know about you, but it is hard to remember what we ate two nights ago, let alone Newtonian physics. Do yourself a favor and take notes, whether on your laptop or in a standard wire bound notebook.

Once you have taken notes, what happens next? It is time to do something with your notes. Of course, you should read them over and review them, but that is not enough. Too often students study by "looking over" their notes. This is a form of passive learning. It is time to engage with learning.

Apply some of these helpful strategies in order to engage with your notes and enhance recall on the exam.

- Transfer your notes onto the Cornell note-taking template.
- Compare your lecture notes to your textbook and add text notes to fill in the gaps. In fact, use a different color pen for your textbook notes.
- Apply the Fold Out strategy to help you compare notes with text. You will be completing a helpful study guide in the process.

- Divide concepts and rewrite notes onto "concept cards." Concept cards are large 5" by 7" index cards which include the term, definition, example, page numbers, diagrams, etc.
- Some people prefer to type their notes after class for readability. This is a great review in itself.

While in Class: Ways to Engage

1. Sit in the front of the classroom or lecture hall.
2. Be prepared. Are there any slides you need to print? Do you have your notebook or binder and a pen (that works)?
3. As cool as your friends are, try not to sit with them or at least let them know you must refrain from banter or gabbing while you take expert notes.
4. Make eye contact with your professor. This lets the professor know you are awake and eager to learn.
5. Avoid Facebook, eBay, or any other inappropriate online material while in lecture class. If the laptop is too distracting, make the right decision and leave it in your bag or at home.
6. Be sure to turn off your cell phone. No one wants to hear your David Guetta ringtone. You are not fooling anyone if you put the phone on vibrate.
7. If your professor talks fast and you cannot keep up, consider purchasing a voice recorder. Be sure to run this by your professor.

Cornell Note-Taking

Cornell notes are a super easy way to organize your lecture notes in terms of the key words, concepts, and theories that the professor will present in class.

a. The first column can be used for key concepts or theories. Key words and concepts are those vocabulary words or theories you will encounter during the lecture. List them here.
b. The second column should be used to take notes on the professor's class lecture. Here you will have a written record of the professor's particular take on the subject matter.
c. Below both columns should be a section dedicated to summary. After each class take the time to summarize the material from the lecture and connect the dots between all of the key words, concepts, and theories that day. Don't just paraphrase!

Each professor is different and because of this, each professor does not present subject material as it is presented in your books and readings. Know their perspective! The lecture notes demand their own special strategy because it is the lecture that the professor will usually draw from most in writing tests and assignments.

Finally, remember that you can customize Cornell notes and play with the formatting. Change the headings, add more sections, or even decorate and doodle in your notes if said decorations and doodles are relevant to the material. Your goal is to learn, but in order to learn, you need to make it enjoyable for yourself. See examples starting on page 34.

Summarization Quick Tips

Did you wake up on the wrong side of the bed this morning? Do you want to learn to summarize more effectively? You may be wondering what the first events of your day have to do with summarizing, but think about it . . . you use summarizing a lot when expressing yourself to others. Let's look back at the first question and think about what kind of day you had.

Let's say that you rolled out of your bed with extreme reluctance, your coffee tasted like mud, you had no hot water, your dog was behaving like Cujo and ripped all your furniture, a robber snuck into your house and stole your breakfast and went to the bathroom on your kitchen floor, and you missed your bus. You arrive late for English 101 and the professor wants you to summarize your morning in a sentence. What do you write? You may not go into grand detail but you may write something similar to this: *My morning was challenging because unexpected and unfortunate events stunted my appreciation for my life at the moment.* Do you think this is an appropriate summarization of your day so far? Discuss why or why not with a partner. To help, think about these qualities that all summaries should have:

- ✔ Must contain the main points of a piece or event. Stating the author's most important idea is crucial for capturing what the author is trying to express. The main idea will most likely be found in the thesis statement.
- ✔ Will be shorter than the original writing or explanation (this is unlike paraphrasing which requires you to put an original piece in your own words and is just as long as the original; think of "summing up" when you hear "summary").
- ✔ Will accurately represent the original meaning.
- ✔ Look for topic sentences to help set a framework or outline for your summary.
- ✔ Be sure that your ideas are in order.
- ✔ Take time to differentiate important information that would make your summary incomplete if not included, and information that is trivial or not essential to paint an accurate picture of what a passage is explaining.

For more information about summarizing, please visit http://owl.english.purdue.edu/owl/

Student Example A

Recall	Notes (in your own words)
	CHAPTER: 4 DATE: Feb 3
Types of Leadership	Motivational Theories
	- Explain how human relations affects motivation.
Pg. 127	Maslow's Hierarchy of Needs (Motivational theroy)
Self-Actualization	1) Physiological Needs → Survival, Food Shelter
Esteem	2) Security Needs → Stability & protection
Social	3) Social Needs → Friendship & companions
Security	4) Esteem Needs → Status & recognition
Physiological	5) Self-Actualization → self-fulfillment
	* Dev. by Abram Maslow
	* MEET LOWER NEEDS 1st
	Theory X → holds that people are naturally irresponsible.
Pg 122	Theory Y → holds that people are naturally self motivated & responsible
Why do some believe in Theroy X and others in Theroy Y?	* Dev. by Douglas McGregor
	* What type of leader you are is determined by which theroy you believe in.

SUMMARY / POSSIBLE TEST QUESTIONS

Motivational theroies explain how & why people are motivated. 2 motivational Theories are Maslow's hierarchy of needs & Theroy X & Y.

In Defense of Food
Chapter 4: Food Science's Golden Age **October 30**

Golden Age Food Science	Scientists were making popular food products contain more nutrients or so we thought. **OUTCOME:** Food with labels saying: low-fat no-cholesterol Foods with additives
Adulterants	**Adulterants Def:** Chemical that should not be combined with other substances; lessen effectiveness of a substance and can be harmful.
1988	**Year of Eating Oat Bran** • Succeeded in getting oat bran into almost all processed food • Set the pattern for manipulating food
Lipophobia	**Lipophobia def:** avoidance of eating fatty foods ***RESULT***
Can food be changed to fit nutritional standards?	**Pigs-** breeding of leaner pigs creating "the NEW white meat" reducing saturated fat intake. **Chickens-** higher levels of omega-3's in yolk by feeding flaxseed to hens
Whole foods in competition with nutritionalism	The sales of whole foods rise and fall as changes are made in the nutritional world because it's much harder to genetically engineer their make-up. Unlike processed foods which can be reformulated at any given time. **EX: Atkins Diet 2003** Breads and pastas were redesigned to fit the diet bearing "low carb" labels; while fresh veggies were left untouched on the engineering end and also on the market shelves.
"Good nutrient" marketing treatment	**Pomegranate-** antioxidants protect against cancer and erectile dysfunction **Walnut-** omega-3 fatty acids act as a defense mechanism for heart disease

Summary
The Golden Age of food science was the start of manipulating the foods we consume to fit the nutrition profile. Just because pork is leaner and higher levels of omega-3 can be found in egg yolks doesn't necessarily mean they are better for you. You receive more nutrients and can prevent disease by consuming natural foods like a walnut.

CHAPTER: DATE:

Summary

The Fold Out Strategy

The Fold Out strategy is a brand new approach to studying! Students can use the Fold Out strategy in two ways:

1. **Before class** while skimming the reading. Key words and definitions are written in the KEY WORD column. Once in class, the student can listen for the key words and add what the professor said about the term. After class, the student completes the ME column.

2. **After class** while reviewing notes. Add to the guide any additional textbook information to fill in the gaps and elaborate on the information.

In both cases, this new strategy helps improve student comprehension of the material. Since it is in a handy format, the Fold Outs are easy to take with you to study on the go. Make one or several for the upcoming exam. Some students prefer to make one for each lecture class. Be sure to make several copies of the Fold Out and keep them in your binder.

How to Fold the Fold Out:

1. Look at the side that says KEY WORDS, PROFESSOR, and ME.

2. Fold the ME column over so that you bend the crease and can still read the KEY WORD column.

3. Next, fold over the KEY WORD column and make a crease. It will start to look like an envelope.

4. Complete the information on the back of the Fold Out so that you know when your next exam will be, what it will cover and your goal grade. Also, complete the information on the flap so you know what content is contained in the guide.

What Goes in Each Section:

KEY WORDS	TEXTBOOK	PROFESSOR	ME
• Bold terms • Italicized terms • Terms the professor repeated more than once • Terms you are unfamiliar with	• Definitions of the key words • Page numbers • Diagrams • Examples • Additional facts	• Examples mentioned in class • Information not covered in the text • Class notes	• Mnemonic devices/ acronyms • Helpful rhymes/ stories that tie the new information to prior knowledge • Notes in your own words

TEXTBOOK

Test Date: ______________

Goal Grade: ______________

Chapters to Study:

What is this thing?

1.) **The Key Word column:** Spend a few minutes skimming the material in your textbook that will be covered in your next class. Use your class syllabus as a guide. Find any words in bold, italics, main headings, and so on that stand out as important. Simply record these words in the key word column and then...

2.) **The Textbook column:** Fold on the line between the PROFESSOR and ME columns so that the TEXTBOOK column magically appears next to the KEY WORD column. *In your own words* write a brief summary of the key terms that you selected. Now you are ready for a fulfilling lecture class.

3.) **The Professor column:** You decide... you can keep the PROFESSOR column open during class or you can take notes the usual way and then transfer what was said in class onto your fold-out after class. Did your professor mention any of the words that you selected? What did the professor say about the key term?

4.) **The Me column:** Now it is your turn. What do you need this column for? More examples, drawings, extra space, to refer to your own life experiences, or maybe even for a mnemonic device or memory aid.

Helpful Hints:

Adapt to your *own* needs. You'll never do the textbook column after class? That's okay, do it afterwards!

Start these early... they'll be helpful study guides.

Draw lines between key terms and/or use color-coding to help you stay focused and on task!

Take them with you on the bus, home, or wherever and use the fold-out a few minutes a day!

Chapter/Concept: ______________

KEY WORDS	PROFESSOR	ME

Concept Cards

What you will need:

- 4×6 or 5×7 (the larger the better)
- Color pens, pencils, or markers
- Textbook, lecture notes, etc

Everyone has used flashcards at least once in their life. If you have tried them in college you may have been unsatisfied with the results come time for an exam. A typical flashcard is made with one word on a side and just the definition on the other, which limits the learner. You may know the definition by heart after studying it several times, but you might not understand what it means. By using concept cards, you can put more information on the card to better understand a term. Not only can you fit a lot of information onto the card, they are easy to carry! You can keep them on you and when you have free time, pull them out and review.

Three Steps to Making and Studying a Concept Card

Step 1: Filtering out the important information. Go over your lecture notes and textbook and compare the bold or italicized words and headings. Professors don't tell you everything in lecture, so it's best to refer to the book to further understand key details.

Step 2: Making the memory cards. Put a word, words or a concept on the front of the card and the supporting information on the other. While you're doing this, make sure to say it out loud to help you remember.

Step 3: Studying the cards. If you need to review the cards in order first, then do so, after that SHUFFLE, SHUFFLE, SHUFFLE! Only pick 5–7 cards at a time, flipping them front to back when reviewing them. Mark a check (if you got the card right) or an X (if you got the card wrong) on the upper right hand corner of the card. Once you get three check marks in a row you know it!

Look on the next page to see an example of a concept card.

DNA Helicase

Def: breaks H bonds between the 2 nucleotide strands of DNA

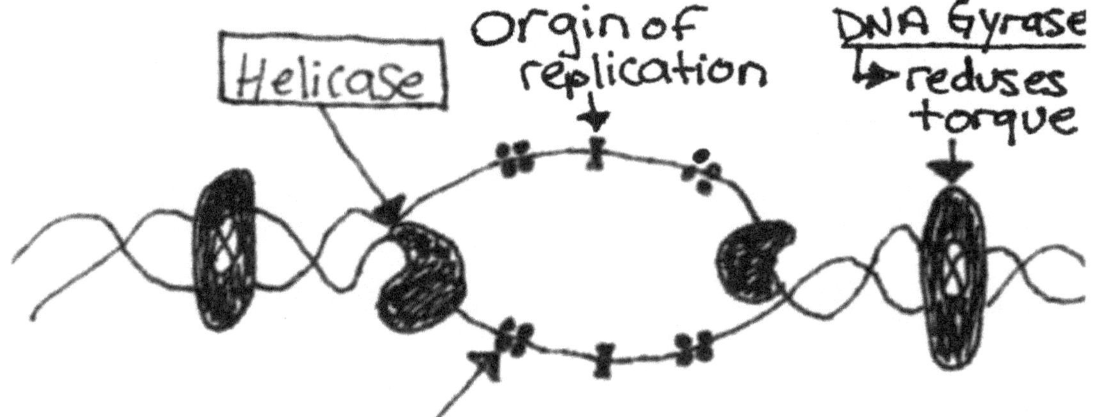

Single Stranded Binding protien:

Prevent Fusing of Complementary Stranc

Note Swap Activity

Directions: "Grade" your peers' notes or your own notes using this quick assessment.

Component	YES	NO
Are the notes legible?		
Is there a date at the top?		
Are the main headings easy to find?		
Are key points underlined/highlighted?		
Can you find any examples?		
Are things abbreviated or paraphrased?		
Are there any diagrams, drawings, page #s?		
Is there any coding (arrows, ? , ! . #)		
Are the notes in a designated binder/notebook?		
Are textbook notes added to lecture notes?		
Total YES:__________		

Multiply the number of YES's times ten. Highest score is 100.

What New Components Will You Include in Your Own Notes?

1.

2.

3.

Discussion: Organization, Studying, and Note-Taking

Whenever I am in class, I tend to write down every single word the professor says. How do I determine what is important to write down?

– Angel

It takes me ten minutes to find anything! This makes me miss out on taking notes. Help!

– Derrick

My exam is in a week. I am used to cramming, but I want to start studying earlier. How do I get started?

– Robin

CHAPTER FOUR:

THE LIBRARY AND YOU

Research and Beyond

"No matter which book you need, it's on the bottom shelf."
–London's Law of Libraries

The University Library is here to Help You!

The Michael Schwartz Library is located in Rhodes Tower. Your Viking card is your library card.

Website: http://library.csuohio.edu
Reference Desk: 216-687-5300

Think of the library as an academic success support center that focuses on providing the tools, resources, and services you need for researching, studying, computing, and connecting.

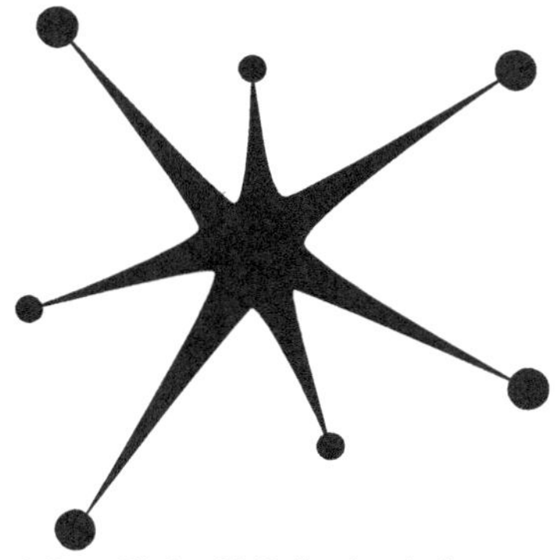

10 Reasons to Use the Michael Schwartz Library

1. Friendly, professional librarians are available to help you with your research.
2. Professor approved sources such as books, e-books, videos, audio recordings, newspapers, magazines, academic journals, and more.
3. Spaces for silent study, group work, meeting friends, and relaxing.
4. Computers with a variety of software and printing are available.

5. You can request books not available at CSU from one of 88 Libraries in Ohio using OhioLINK.
6. You can borrow still or video cameras and audio recorders from Multi Media Services.
7. Lockers are available to rent for a small fee.
8. InterLibrary Loan (ILL) can be used to obtain articles that are not available at CSU.
9. Popular books and magazines for recreational reading are available in the Cleveland Public Library collection.
10. Your friends are here!

What is Information Literacy? Why is it Important?

Simply stated, "Information Literacy is the set of skills needed to find, retrieve, analyze, and use information." [1]

Regardless of your major or the courses you take, you will need to use information literacy skills to be successful in your academic work and in your professional career after graduation.

Before you start your research, determine what information you need to find.

- Read through your assignment and determine your professor's expectations.
- Ask questions if anything is unclear.
- Identify an area of interest and narrow down to a manageable topic.
- Write out your research question or preliminary thesis.
- Brainstorm a list of search terms, key concepts, and questions. Try using a mind map to organize your ideas.

Determine the best search tools to help you locate sources and start searching.

- Use WorldCat@CSU, Scholar online catalog, OhioLINK, and the research databases provided by the library.
- Visit, call, or email the library and ask a librarian to help you get started.
- When creating search statements, try different word combinations using similar, related terms.

---

[1] American Library Association. "Introduction to Information Literacy." http://www.ala.org/acrl/issues/infolit/overview/intro

- Search for a variety of source types and formats.
- Be sure to seek out differing viewpoints about your topic to ensure you are well informed.
- Make sure you have enough sources to answer your research question(s).

Frequently Asked Questions

What is WorldCat@CSU?

It is a search tool that provides single-search-box access to millions of items from authoritative content sources available at CSU libraries as well as libraries in Ohio and the world.

What is Scholar Online Catalog?

Scholar is a library catalog. It is a descriptive list of items that are owned by a particular library. Library catalogs are electronic information databases accessed by computer and called "online catalogs."

What is OhioLINK?

The Ohio Library and Information Network, OhioLINK, is a consortium of 88 Ohio college and university libraries, and the State Library of Ohio, that work together to provide Ohio students, faculty, and researchers with the information they need for teaching and research. Serving more than 600,000 students, faculty, and staff at 89 institutions, OhioLINK's membership includes 16 public/research universities, 23 community/technical colleges, 49 private colleges, and the State Library of Ohio.[2]

What is a Research Database?

Research databases allow you to use keyword searching to locate information about articles that have been published in journals, magazines, and newspapers. Some research databases also provide access to book reviews, film reviews, dramas, financial reports, and many other sources of information. Many of the articles listed in the databases are available in full-text format. Full-text means the entire text of the article is available online. You can read, print, or email the article directly from the computer.

What is a Library PIN?

PINs are used by the CSU Libraries to ensure the privacy of your library account.

You create your own PIN. The use of PINs ensures that you, and only you, have access to the information maintained in your library account. You will be prompted for your PIN when checking your

[2]OhioLINK website http://www.ohiolink.edu/about/what-is-ol.html

library account or renewing books in Scholar. Your PIN also will be required when you connect to research databases or electronic books from home. You will not need your PIN for just searching the online catalog.

Go here to set up your PIN: https://scholar.csuohio.edu/patroninfo~S0

What is an Annotated Bibliography?

An annotated bibliography is a document that lists the citations to books, articles, and other potential sources for your research paper or project. Each source's citation is followed by an annotation—a brief paragraph that describes and evaluates the source. The annotation should inform the reader about the relevance, accuracy, and quality of the sources cited.

Need Help With Your Annotated Bibliography Assignment?

You will be visiting the library with your class. During the visit, you will learn more about the annotated bibliography and develop valuable skills to help you complete the assignment. You will also want to check out the online research guide for ASC 101: http://researchguides.csuohio.edu/asc101

Evaluate and Document Your Sources!

- **CURRENCY:** Is the material current? Does it contain outdated or disproven information? Is the site updated regularly?
- **RELEVANCE:** Does the source answer your questions? Does it provide useful information? Is it too complicated to understand or too elementary?
- **AUTHORITY:** Who is the author? What can you find out about them? Can you determine their credentials? Are they a qualified expert? Is the author's contact info listed?

© RetroClipArt, 2012. Used under license from Shutterstock, Inc.

- **ACCURACY:** What evidence does the author use? Are facts documented? Is there a bibliography?
- **PURPOSE:** Why was the information created: to inform, to sell, to persuade? Is it fact or opinion? Is the information biased?

Learn to Determine the Differences Between Popular, Trade, and Scholarly Publications.

Not all articles are created equal. There are specific qualities that distinguish articles published in popular magazines and newspapers, trade journals, and scholarly journals. Be sure that the type of article you are using matches your professor's expectations and your research needs.

What Does Peer Reviewed or Refereed Mean?

Peer Review is a process that journal publishers use to ensure the articles they publish represent the best scholarship currently available. When an article is submitted to a peer reviewed journal, the editors send it out to other scholars in the same field (the author's peers) to get their opinion on the quality of the scholarship, its relevance to the field, its appropriateness for the journal, etc.

Publications that do not use peer review (i.e., *Time, Newsweek, Salon*) just rely on the judgment of the editors. That's why you can't count on them for solid, scientific scholarship.

CRITERIA	POPULAR	TRADE	SCHOLARLY
Appearance	eye-catching cover; glossy paper; color pictures and illustrations; each issue starts with page number 1	cover depicts industrial setting; glossy paper; color pictures and illustrations; each issue starts with page number 1	plain cover; plain paper; black and white graphics and illustrations; consecutive pagination throughout each volume
Audience	nonprofessionals	members of a specific business, industry, or organization	researchers and professionals
Content	personalities, news and general interest articles; articles written by staff, may be unsigned	industry trends, new products or techniques, and organizational news; articles written by staff and contributing authors	research projects, methodology, and theory; article written by contributing authors; authors are professionals and researchers in the field
Accountability	editorial review	editorial review; may have short bibliographies	peer reviewed, refereed; extensive bibliographies
Advertisements	heavy	moderate; all or most are trade related	few or none
Examples	*Gourmet* *Newsweek* *Psychology Today* *Time*	*Chilton's Food Engineering* *Public Management* *APA Monitor* *Advertising Age*	*Journal of Food Science* *Urban Studies* *Journal of Applied Psychology* *Journal of Extension*

Document Your Sources.

- Make sure you identify and record all the publication information for any sources you might use.
- Know which citation style (i.e., MLA, APA) your professor wants you to use. Different disciplines use different styles. For example, English uses MLA and Psychology typically uses APA.
- Cite everything you quote directly from a source or any ideas you paraphrase.
- Make an appointment at the CSU Writing Center if you have questions or need help citing.
- Create an annotated bibliography to help you organize your sources.

Discussion: Library Skills

My friend goes to school here too and he said in two years he has not been to the library. He is about to be dismissed from the university, but is it true I can do all my research online?

– Jake

When I am doing my research I have a hard time determining credible sources. What are some things to look for?

– Erin

On my last English paper I changed all the words from my sources, but I still got in trouble for plagiarizing. How do I avoid this in the future?

– Ben

CHAPTER FIVE:

GET INTO IT!

Active Reading

"You cannot open a book without learning something." –Confucius

© RetroClipArt, 2012. Used under license from Shutterstock, Inc.

As college students you encounter reading in every course you take. Many of you are shocked by the homework expectations. In the first four weeks of a term, it is not unusual for professors to assign 70 pages of reading each time the class meets. College level courses typically have two to four exams which will be based on 200 to 400 pages of reading in addition to lecture material. It is easy to see how study time begins to add up.

Fellow students have asked . . .

"I have read for three hours straight and cannot remember a thing. What should I do?"

You are not alone. Many students put in the time required, diligently read the assigned chapters, and understand the author's points. Yet when asked to recall information from the reading, they cannot provide specific details.

You need to be an active reader. Do something with the information you read. Attending lecture or looking at words on a written page does not create meaning. Take notes, look for the main idea and define vocabulary. While reading, reflect on what was written and then try to apply the concepts to your life. Make the information meaningful to you—especially if it does not seem to apply to your life. Information that is not used is more likely to be forgotten as soon as you close the book. To truly understand the meaning of what you are reading, you need to interact with what is read.

"I will never finish this!"

So you have eight chapters to read and it is two nights before the exam. Don't panic. Make a plan instead.

1. Determine exactly how many pages you will be reading. How long will this take you to read and comprehend the material?
2. Break the reading up into smaller time slots. Take short 5–10 minute breaks in between each section. Review what you read before the break and then begin the new section.
3. Review pictures and information in the margins.
4. Skim through the information discussed in class, slowing down to cover confusing topics.
5. Carefully read new material not covered in class, using active reading strategies.
6. Create one or two questions for each section that might be on the test.

"I just read the chapter and do not understand anything I read. Buying the book was a waste of money; I do not even read it anymore."

First of all, you need an attitude change. Tell yourself, "I am going to read this and remember it." You can do it; it's all about focus and positive thinking. If you say you cannot do it, you will never succeed.

Think about what you already know by using a KWL map (Know, Wonder, Learn) for assistance. In the left column (**K**now), write the facts you know about the topic. In the middle column (**W**onder), answer the question, "What do I want to know about this topic," or write questions you want to answer while you read. Finally, when you have completed a section (not the entire chapter), write down the answers to your questions (**L**earned). See the example started below.

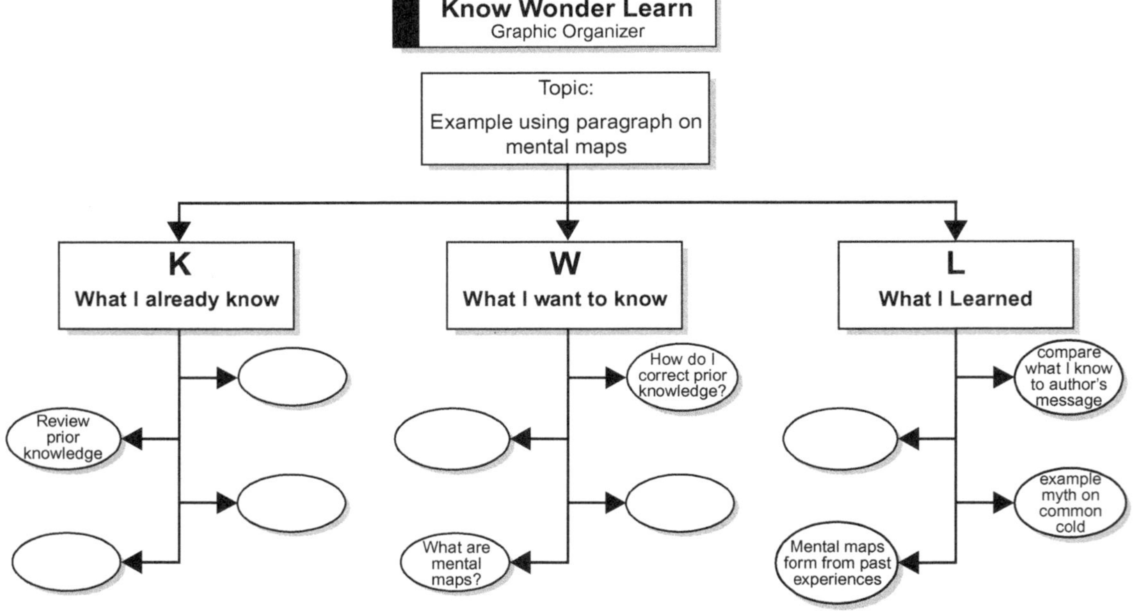

If you are still struggling: SEEK OUT HELP! Contact your professor and ask specific questions, go to TASC and sign up for tutoring, or study with a friend who is willing to help you understand the material. Do not give up.

Past Experiences Form Your Mental Map

Everyone has their own mental map of the world. Your past experiences create your knowledge, or what you know about the subjects. When you read, you compare what the author is saying to your own mental map. What you take away from the text can be totally different from your best friend. There are also times when you need to change your perception of the topic to understand what the author is trying to tell you. If your prior perception is not altered, you will have trouble constructing meaning using the new information. To be successful at reading, you need to use the correct prior knowledge and the necessary processing strategies to comprehend the author's message. Only you can comprehend and use the information. Your friend cannot do it for you. This is why you may have trouble reading a nuclear fusion book while your friend breezes through it.

To understand how important your mental map is to reading try the exercise below.

1. Read the following passage. As you read it, examine what your brain is doing to understand it, and decide upon a title for the passage.

    Title ____

    Consider using different types for different populations and environments. You can buy them at a specialty shop or find them on your own. Some people prefer the fake ones, but they don't always work as well. They seem to have a sixth sense and can tell when it isn't real. In addition, they can often smell you on it and this alerts them to stay away. Try using gloves when you handle them. However, when there is a dense population it doesn't seem to matter as much. Just make sure it looks alive when it moves. Depending on the size, you may need to cut it into pieces and thread it through the center of each piece, letting parts of them dangle from the sides. You can also use several whole pieces depending on the size of your equipment. If you use a big one, thread the entire segment, letting the end hang off. Whatever the size, make sure it is secure.

2. What was your brain doing while you were reading?

3. Why did you find it hard to grasp? What is missing that caused you to have trouble understanding the author's message?

4. What did you do to help yourself construct meaning? What fix-it strategies did you try to use to help you understand?

Did you encounter this while reading?

As I read the passage, I was able to decode the words but not understand the sentence. When I tried to compare my previous knowledge on the subject to the author's message, something was wrong. I noticed the pronouns in the passage were not clear, which made reading the passage confusing. I struggled to find meaning and finally gave up. The strategies I tried did not work and I decided I did not need to know the information.

What if you knew that the passage was about fishing worms? Would this information help you understand the author's message? Why?

5. Reread the passage, it should be easier to read this time!

The second time through the paragraph, you were able to draw on your own mental map of how to bait a fishing hook using worms. Even if you have never fished, your brain had some picture of how this process was to occur. This prior picture and the new information contained in the passage allowed you to create a new mental map. This, in the end, allowed you to actively read what the author was telling you.

Highlight Much?

Ever look over your text book and realize that you highlighted all but two words on a page? Are your markers running as dry as dust? Do you wish you were color blind and could not work with bright colors anymore? If any of these questions apply to you or if you are looking for ideas about effective underlining and highlighting skills while studying, there are tips to proactively change the way you mark and distinguish the pertinent information of class material.

- **Know your limit!** Setting a cap on how much you plan on distinguishing information that you want to reference for later may help avoid the highlighting crazies. Just like with summarizing or paraphrasing, there are reasons why condensing material is friendly to your brain and your ability to remember key concepts. Some study experts (didn't even know there was such a thing) recommend limiting your markings to once or twice per paragraph. This is because reading is an active learning process and highlighting is a visual and physical cue to your brain to recognize the importance of what you marked.
- **The only time you don't have to mark the thesis!** Although detecting the author's thesis is essential in determining the author's main idea, you do not automatically mark it for this reason. Often the thesis is not as useful as the real-world examples the text gives. These application phrases or sentences show rather than tell.
- **Vary your markings:** Stripes of color aren't the only visuals you may put down on paper! Try developing your own secret code of organizing key ideas by indicating what type of information you mean to record. For example, you may want to underline phrases, box key words, or put asterisks next to a larger section you want to identify.
- **Your chance to edit:** Before you think "wait that is not my job" consider the goal of editing: to figuratively weed out and dig up the core ideas the author is communicating. This will help you get to the point and be selective while reading, allowing you to have a deeper and more thorough understanding of the important concepts.
- **Try other modes of transportation:** Think about expanding your means of marking by using supplies other than highlighters to allow for more variety (and ease for your eyes).

Annotating in five easy steps

Sometimes you have no prior knowledge on a subject or your prior mental map is not totally correct. An example of this would be the first time you read a history book. The events, dates, and times can become confusing and difficult to sort out; however, if you just move on, the information would be lost. Again, you need to interact with the information by annotating your textbook. Yes, this means writing in the textbook. To truly understand new concepts, you need to mark up the textbook. The strategy contains five steps that, with practice, will become a natural habit.

Annotating in five easy steps

1. Find short phrases that succinctly express the main idea. Draw a box around it and write Main Idea.
2. Find brief definitions. Circle the terms, underline the definition, and write "DEF" in the margin.
3. Write ex (for example) in the margins next to any example or illustration.
4. Put a ? next to things you do not understand.
5. Put an ! next to things you think are important.

You do not always have to do all the above. It will depend on what you are reading. In four to six weeks of continued use, you will annotate without thinking about the steps. Give it some time and try it out.

Without review, annotating is a waste of time. After the completion of reading the page, chapter or passage, do not forget to complete this last step. Imagine you will be tested on this passage. Write two test questions based on the passage. Find the answer to the questions using the annotations you made while reading.

Let's try this out on the passage below.

Read the paragraph from Michael Pollan's book *In Defense of Food* (pages 70–72). The passage discusses how to study the impact of diet on health.

As you read, mark the passage using the five steps for annotating.

"But if confounding factors of lifestyle bedevil epidemiological comparisons of different populations, the supposedly more rigorous studies of large American populations suffer from their own arguably even more disabling flaws. In ascending order of supposed reliability, nutrition researchers have three main methods for studying the impact of diet on health: the case-control study, the cohort study, and the intervention trail. All three are seriously flawed in different ways.

In the case-control study, researchers attempt to determine the diet of a subject who has been diagnosed with a chronic disease in order to uncover its cause. One problem is that when people get sick they may change the way they eat, so the diet they report may not be the diet responsible for their illness. Another problem is that the patients will typically report eating large amounts of whatever the evil nutrient of the moment is. . . .

. . . Long-term observational studies of cohort groups such as the Nurses' Health Study represent a big setup in the reliability from the case-control study. For one thing the studies are prospective rather than retrospective. They begin tracking subjects before they become ill."

Michael Pollan. 2008. *In Defense of Food: An Eater's Manifesto.* (Kindle Location 914). Penguin Group. Kindle Edition.

Imagine you are in a nutrition class. What two questions might be on the test based on the passage?

1.

2.

How does yours compare to the one below?

"But if confounding factors of lifestyle bedevil epidemiological comparisons of different populations, the supposedly more rigorous studies of large American populations suffer from their own arguably even more disabling flaws. In ascending order of supposed reliability, nutrition researchers have three main methods for studying the impact of diet on health: the case-control study, the cohort study, and the intervention trail. All three are seriously flawed in different ways.

Main Idea

In the case-control study, researchers attempt to determine the diet of a subject who has been diagnosed with a chronic disease in order to uncover its cause. One problem is that when people get sick they may change the way they eat, so the diet they report may not be the diet responsible for their illness. Another problem is that the patients will typically report eating large amounts of whatever the evil nutrient of the moment is...

!

...Long-term observational studies of cohort groups such as the Nurses' Health Study represent a big setup in the reliability from the case-control study. For one thing the studies are prospective rather than retrospective. They begin tracking subjects before they become ill.

EX

Imagine you are taking a nutrition class. What two questions might be on the test based on the passage?

1. Discuss the flaws of the case-control study and its impact on the participants diet and health.

2. Which of the studies is the most reliable? Why?

Concept Mapping

Think You're a "Visual Learner"?

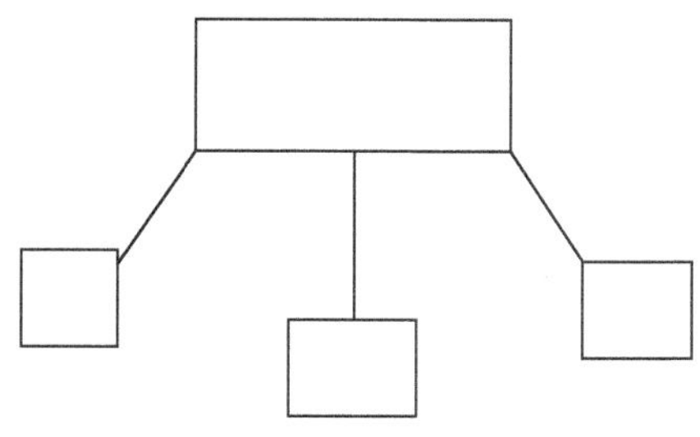

If so, this is the PERFECT study tool for you! Concepts maps are a FUN way to study. When you make studying fun, you will retain the information you need to know. Maps give you an opportunity to connect concepts in your own way by using colors or drawing pictures in an organized fashion. REMEMBER: this is a study tool for YOU so you can be as creative as you want!

***BONUS of CONCEPT MAPPING:** becoming an active learner!

What you will need:

- Blank, white or color paper
- Color pencils, pens or markers
- Textbook
- Lecture notes

Guidelines For Creating a Concept Map

1. Take out your textbook or lecture notes and look for bold words or phrases.
2. Pull out ALL the information that revolves around that key word or phrase.
3. Get your blank paper and put the word or phrase in a box at the top. This will be your main idea for your concept map.
4. Take the additional information and start branching off of your main idea.
5. When you have completed your concept map, you should be able to look at it and explain why the boxes or pictures connect in the way that you have created.

Student Example A

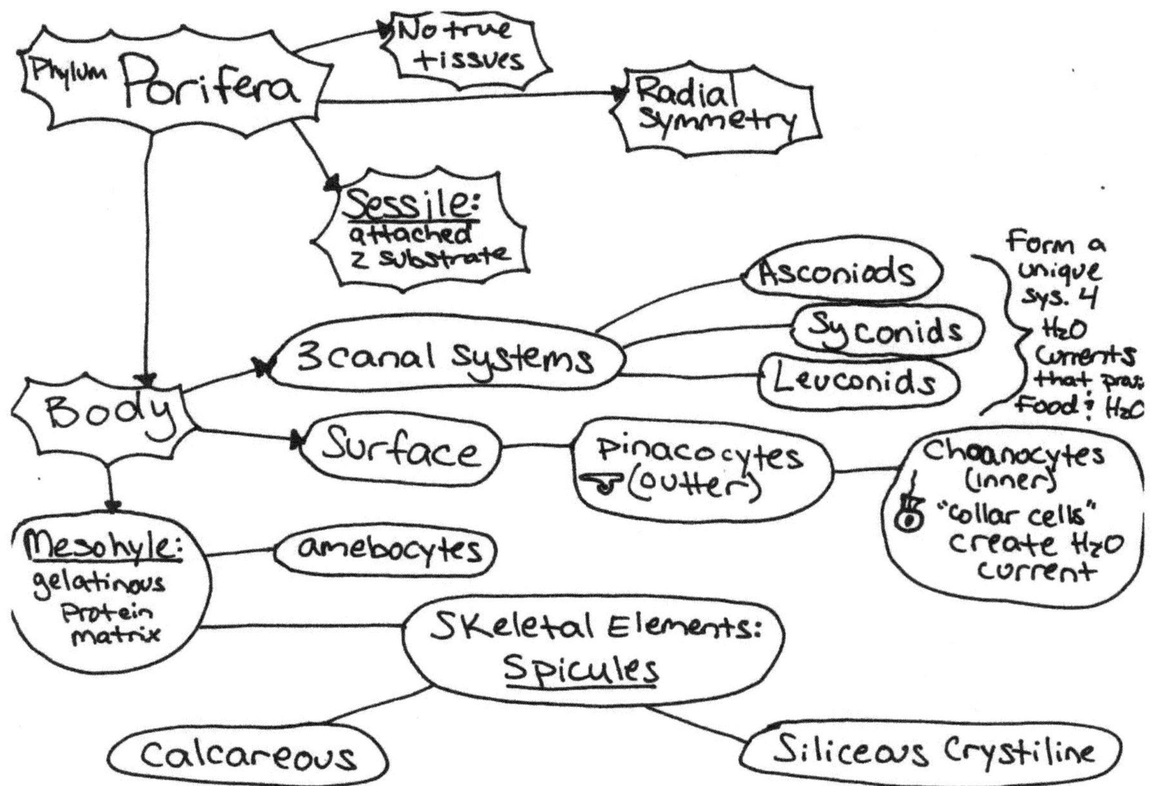

Student Example B

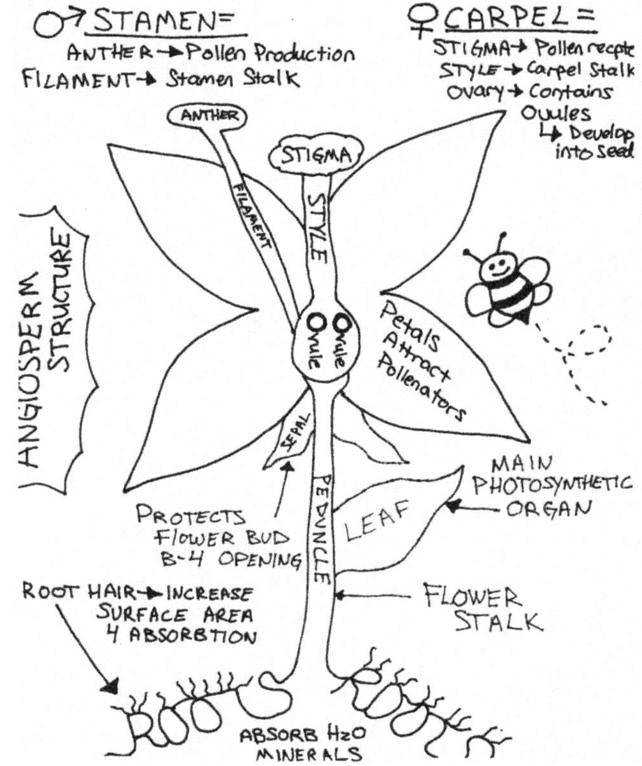

Graphic Organizers

If you are not into creating your own map or want to try something different, try one of the featured graphic organizers on the next few pages. While you are reviewing the different options, you may be wondering which one to choose.

1. **KWL (Know, Wonder, Learn)** — This is a great organizer to use before, during, after class, or preparing for the test.

   Before class — Under the **Know** column write down everything you already know about the topic. In the **Wonder** column create questions that need further explanation or should be answered in class.

   During class — Keep the chart close at hand and highlight the questions and information in your chart.

   After class — Compare your notes and the chart. Add material from your notes to the chart, answer the questions, add new questions, and cross off any incorrect information. Look at the information that is not highlighted. Ask yourself, "Do I need to know this? Is it in the reading from the textbook?" If you do not need to know it, cross it off.

   Preparing for a test — Using a blank form, fill in all the columns with what you learned about the topic. Any questions that cannot be answered or topics with only minor details need to be looked at again.

2. **Compare and Contrast** — This is a great organizer to use when first sorting out unfamiliar information. Also consider using this when you are studying for the exam to test your knowledge; or use it when preparing for a paper in which you must describe both sides.

3. **Main Ideas** — Using your notes, create this graphic organizer to show the important information about the topic. This will help create a visual image which you will recall in your mind during the exam. Feel free to branch off on your own ideas and add to the template.

4. **Study Guide Map** — Instead of rereading your notes, create your own study guide. Actively using information will assist you in recalling it during the exam.

5. **Break it Down** — When studying for exams, choose this graphic organizer to expand your knowledge of a specific topic and to learn the related vocabulary. Another use is to narrow your topic before writing a paper.

In which class would you use each of these graphic organizers?

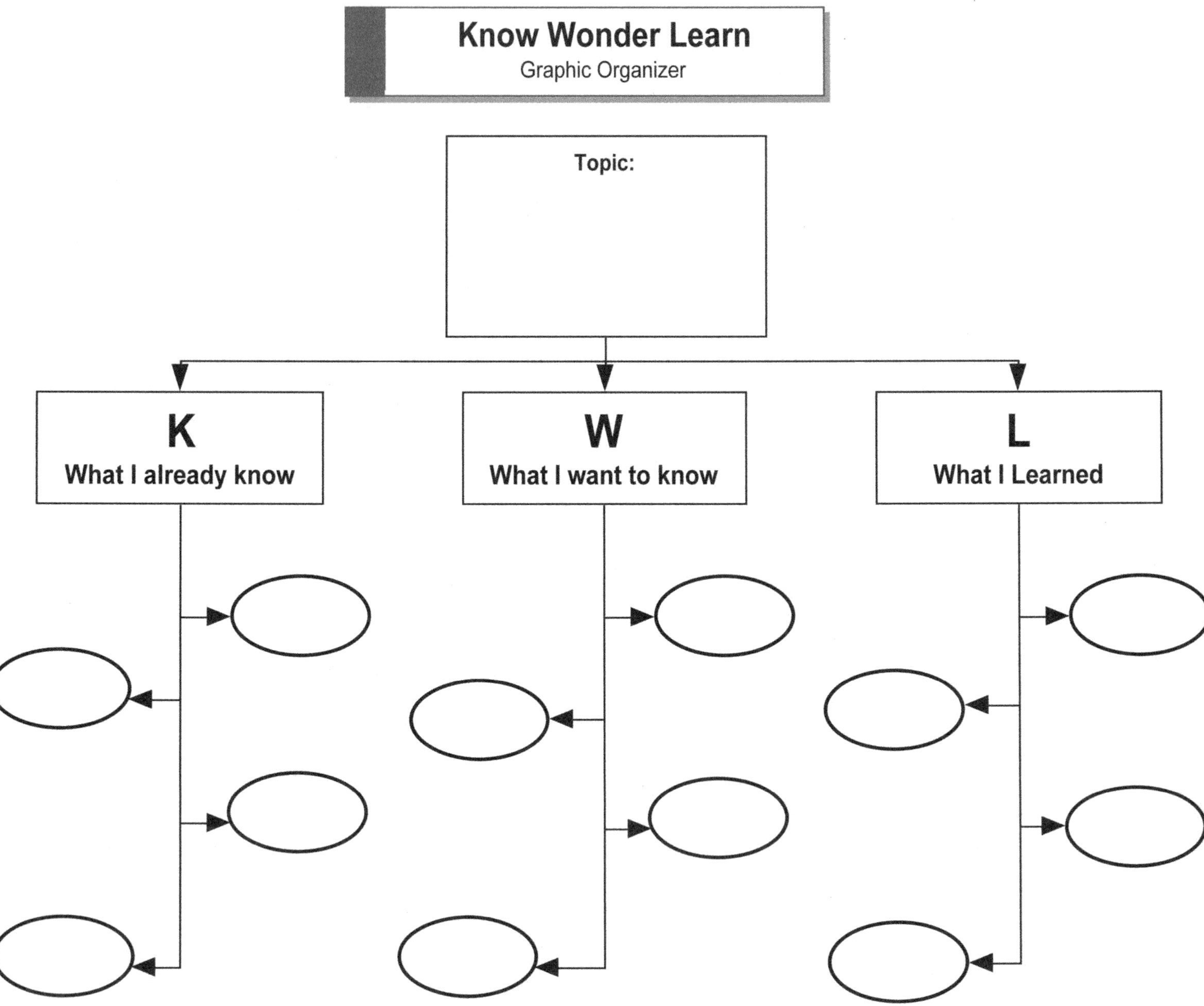
Know Wonder Learn
Graphic Organizer
Topic:
K
What I already know
W
What I want to know
L
What I Learned

Compare and Contrast

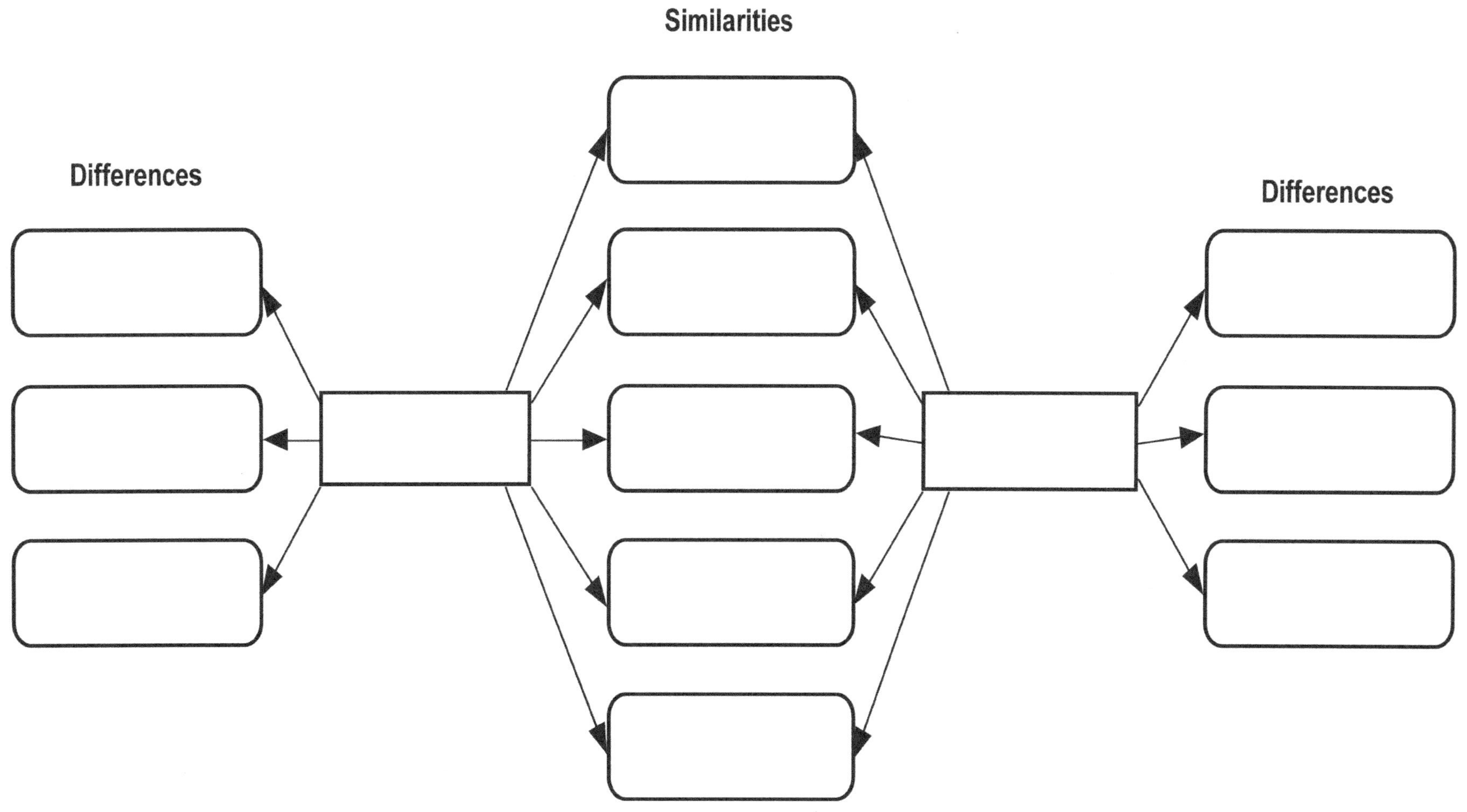

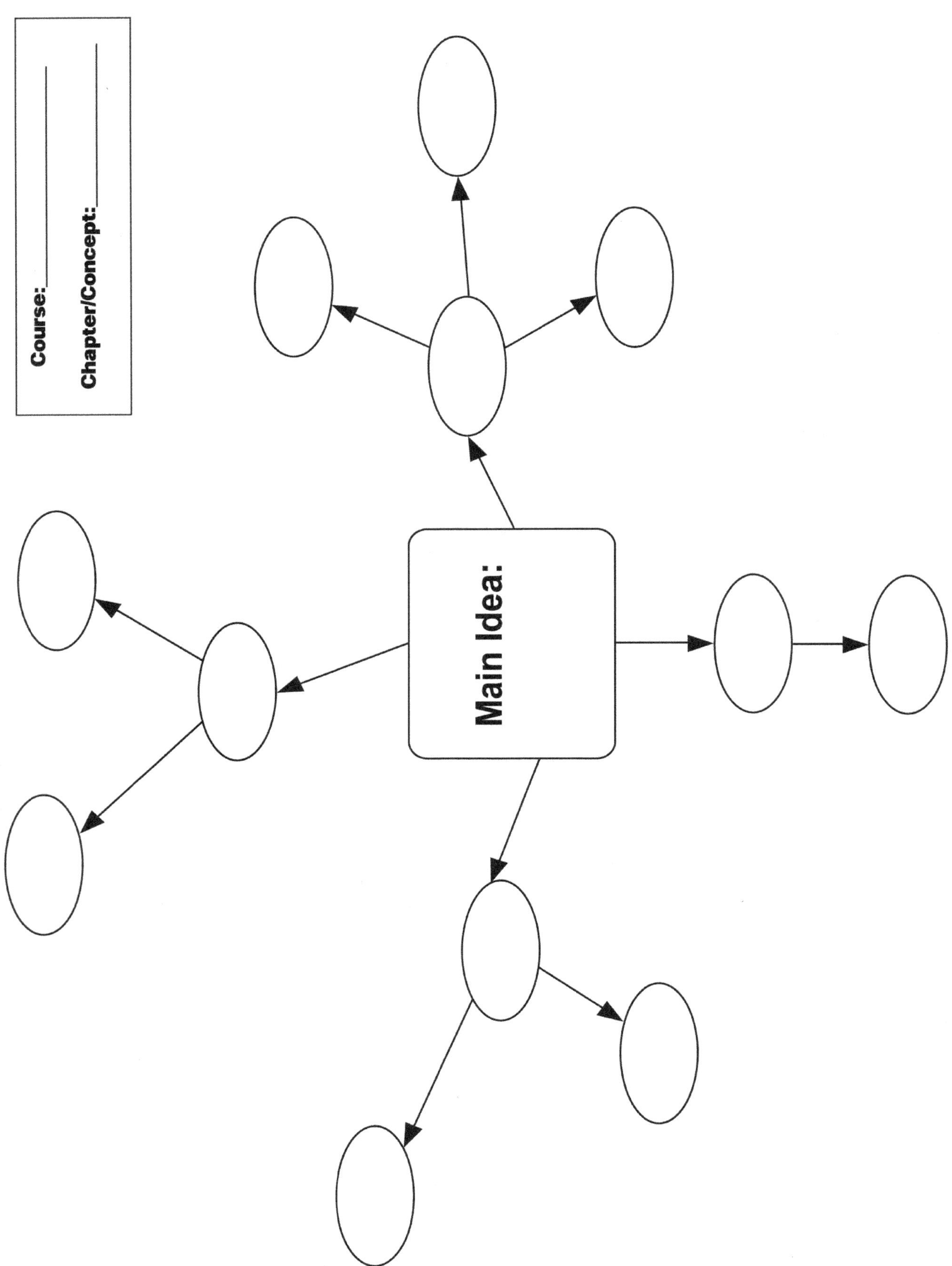
Course:
Chapter/Concept:
Main Idea:

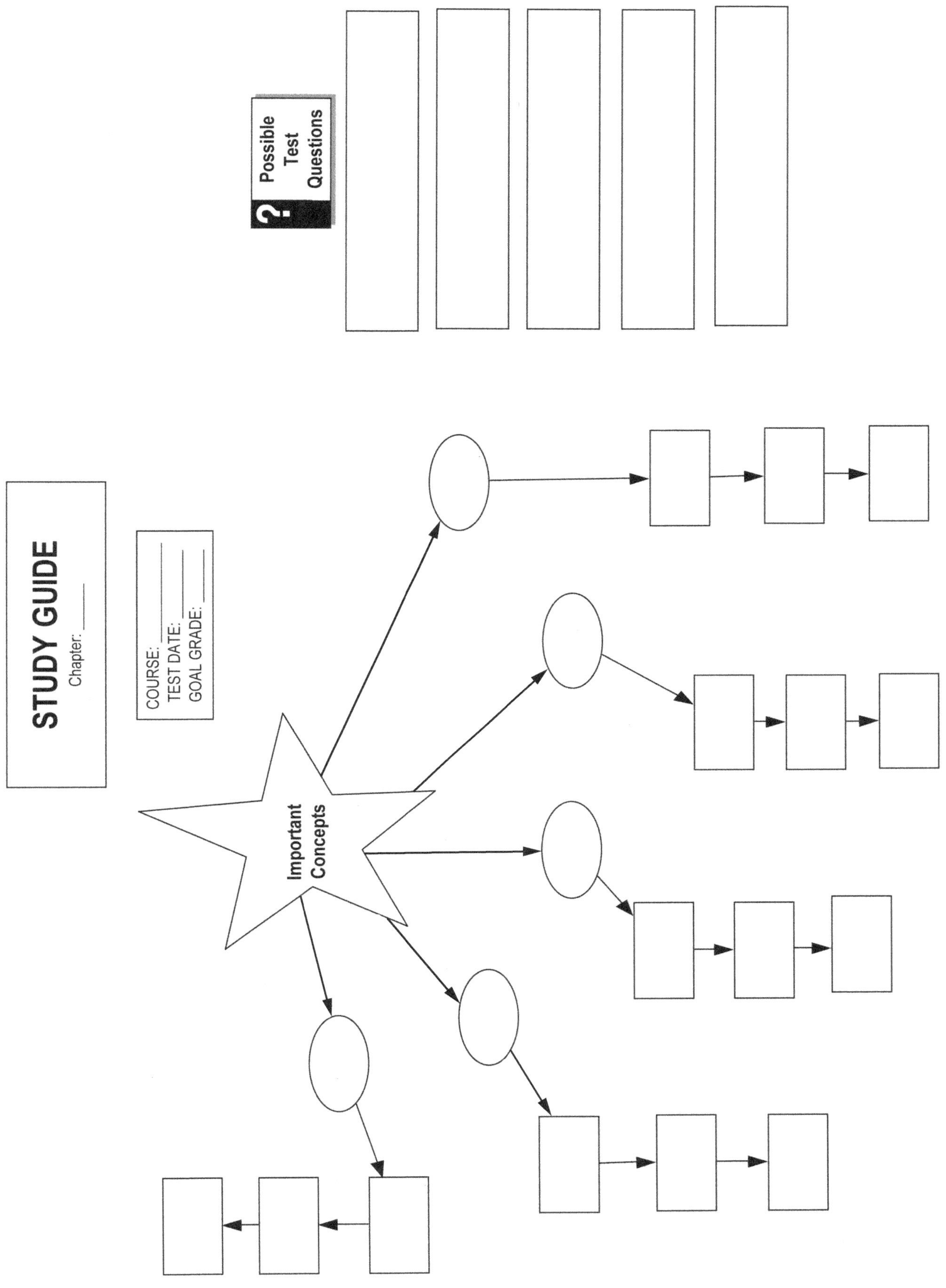
STUDY GUIDE
Chapter: ____
COURSE: ____
TEST DATE: ____
GOAL GRADE: ____
Important Concepts
? Possible Test Questions

Break it Down

Take tough concepts and make them more comprehendible with this graphic organizer!

Discuss and List Five Important Concepts
1. 2. 3. 4. 5.
Choose One Concept and Relate Four Ideas
1. 2. 3. 4.
Choose and Define Three New Words
1. 2. 3.
In Your own Words Discuss Two Concepts or Ideas You Already Knew
1. 2.
Write One Question You Still Have
1.

Discussion: Active Reading

I disagree with the author's view. It makes reading this book really hard. I also think my professor doesn't value my comments if they do not agree with hers. Help!

– Taylor

I find marking the important information difficult using my iPad. Are there any features or shortcuts that would help me?

– Anthony

I was told by the bookstore that I can write in my textbooks and still return them as long as it is in pencil and not too excessive. Knowing this, how should I proceed marking my textbook?

– Damian

CHAPTER SIX:

MAJOR DECISIONS

"What do I want to be when I . . .?" —*Unknown*

You tell everyone you have decided to attend Cleveland State University and the first response and question you probably hear is, "Awesome! What is your major?" For some students, this is an easy question to answer. For others, the thought of choosing a major is overwhelming.

Perhaps you fit into one of the following categories:

- ☐ **Undecided**—*I marked undecided on my admission application for major.*
  (Note: 30% of incoming freshman students who are admitted to Cleveland State University mark this on their application.)

© PHOTOBUAY, 2012. Used under license from Shutterstock, Inc.

- ☐ **Obligated to make a decision**—*I felt obligated to choose a major so I marked _________. Now I have no interest in that major.*
- ☐ **Mid semester change**—*I thought I would like ________ as a major. I went to see my advisor and have changed majors.*
- ☐ **I knew it all along**—*I knew my major in high school and am very happy with my choice.*

Am I on the Right Track?

Yes, all the students above are on the right track. During your freshman year and even up to 60 credit hours, it is OK to change your major. The sooner you find the one that fits you, the easier it will be to complete your degree in four years. As long as you keep your advisor informed and let them assist you in making the correct choice for you, they will guide you down the path to earning your degree.

What is a Major?

Your major should be something you are passionate about. It is also the area of study that you are most focused on in college. Some examples of majors are Electrical Engineering, Nursing, Marketing, Economics, and Middle Childhood Education.

How do I Start?

Look at your personal values by considering these questions.

> *Where do you want to work? What hours do you want to work? Do you have a desire to travel in your job? Do you like to work with people or do you prefer to work in a lab with data? Just because a friend or family member says this is a great career does not mean it is the one for you.*

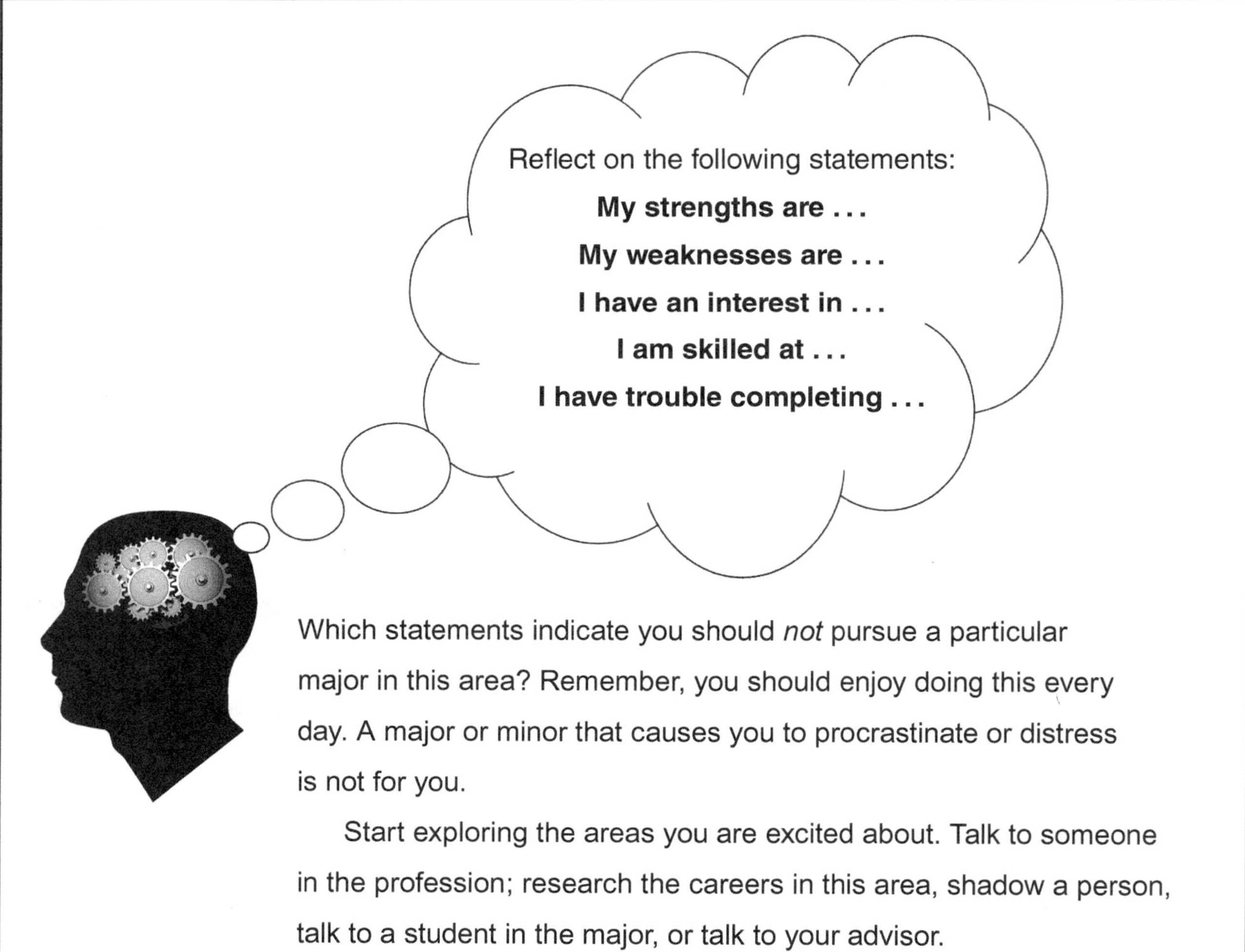

Which statements indicate you should *not* pursue a particular major in this area? Remember, you should enjoy doing this every day. A major or minor that causes you to procrastinate or distress is not for you.

Start exploring the areas you are excited about. Talk to someone in the profession; research the careers in this area, shadow a person, talk to a student in the major, or talk to your advisor.

Work Value Inventory

When considering a major, think about the values you want in your career after you graduate. Is family time important? Do you want a job where you travel? What is important to you?

List 8 values that are important to you when choosing a major and later in a career.

1.
2.
3.
4.
5.
6.
7.
8.

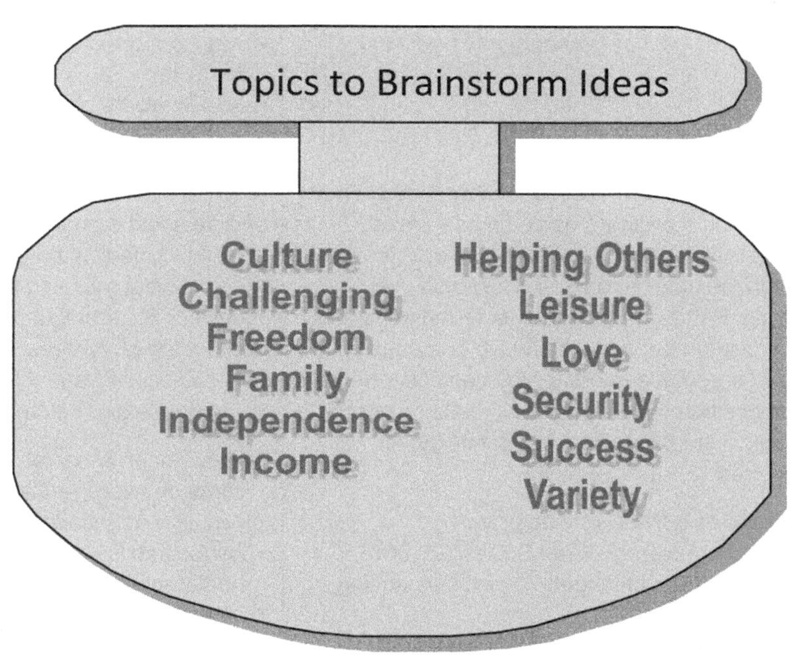

Based on the Daniel E. Super's Work Value Inventory (1970) and the Maryland Work Value Inventory

Questions to Consider

How well do your values correspond to a major in Psychology or Allied Health?

What values from these job descriptions match your values?

Psychology Major	Admissions Counselor Responsible for the recruitment and enrollment of students to a college or university. Admission Counselors are typically assigned to a particular geographic territory. The Counselor will balance his/her efforts between individual entrepreneurship and support of the admissions team. You can also pursue this position with a degree in education, higher education administration, or counseling. • Requires a bachelor's degree • Earns on average $45,000 • Requires good listening skills and the ability to be aware of the reactions of others • Requires good negotiating skills • Value: independence—able to decide how to get something done without the significant direction from someone else • Value: help others • Requires a lot of overnight and weekend travel	Employee Training Instructor They develop course materials and train employees in job skills and decision making skills needed to enhance their job performance and career development within an organization. They select and develop teaching aids. Assess trainees to determine their skill level and their training needs. You can also pursue this position with a degree in education, human resources, business, or organizational administration and leadership. • Requires a bachelor's or master's degree • Earns on average $39,000–$68,000 • Requires you to give speeches and talk to groups of people, to teach others, and use logic to identify strengths and weaknesses of solutions • Leads others • Value: help others • Spends a great deal of time on phone and computer • Usually works Monday–Friday, 8–5
Allied Health Major	Cardiologist Cardiologists treat diseases of the heart. They use electrocardiograms and miniaturized cameras inserted into the heart's arteries to diagnose heart problems. They also use physical stress tests to measure the impact of exercise on the patient's heart. They decide if heart surgery is needed. You can also pursue this position with bachelors in biology, or pre-medical studies. Additional schooling is required. • Requires a Ph. D or Doctorate • Earns on average $200,000–$300,000 • Requires troubleshooting, problem solving, and science skills • Accuracy is a must in this profession. There are serious consequences for errors made. • Values: help others, high income, independence, prestige • Will be exposed to diseases and infections • Hours vary. Works nights and weekends.	Medical Insurance Claims Analyst Medical insurance claims analysts evaluate and decide the amount of insurance benefits to be paid to medical patients based upon the medical diagnosis and treatments they received. For ambiguous medical cases, they contact the physicians, hospitals, or patients. You can also pursue this position with a degree in insurance and risk management. • Requires an associate or bachelor's degree • Earns on average $30,000–$45,000 • Requires negotiating and persuasion skills • Value: stability—duties of job are stable and predictable • On the phone and computer most of the day • Will be put in situations with potential conflict • Typically works Monday–Friday, 8–5

Questions to Consider

For each of the scenarios below:

What are the student's strengths and weaknesses?

What skills does the student possess?

What ideals are important to the student?

What major should the student consider?

Scenario 1: Lorna's Dilemma

© nuttakit, 2012. Used under license from Shutterstock, Inc.

Lorna is a full time student living in the residence halls. After two years of college, she has narrowed down her major to music and engineering. All her general education requirements have been completed and it is time to make the choice. When choosing general education courses she completed several of the courses in music, math and physics. Growing up, Lorna enjoyed taking courses in math and science. She enjoyed the discovery of new ideas. To her, math and science were easy to understand and apply to new concepts. She spent her summers playing in a jazz band for local summer festivals. In school she was involved in band and jazz band. She practiced hours on several instruments and always brought home top honors when entered into a school instrumental contest. Lorna enjoys taking her family's old equipment apart to see how it works.

Lorna cannot decide which major to choose. She enjoys both music and engineering. Lorna is living in the residence halls to become independent, even though her family is 30 minutes away. She wants to have a secure future that involves doing interesting work. Lorna does not want a job that does the same thing day after day. She wants to do something that makes a difference but also allows her to relax and do things she enjoys outside of work.

Questions to Consider

For each of the scenarios below:

What are the student's strengths and weaknesses?

What skills does the student possess?

What ideals are important to the student?

What major should the student consider?

Scenario 2: Enrique's Dilemma

Enrique and Rita married young and have two children ages six and eight. Spending time with their children and family are important to both of them. For the last several years, Enrique has been working full time to support his family and to provide an income while Rita attended college to complete her degree. It is now Enrique's time to finish his education. He plans on working full time and going to school part time. Rita's new job requires her to travel several weeks out of the year. During these times, Enrique is both father and mother to the children, on top of work and school. Enrique was able to complete the courses and practicum experience to work as a lab assistant at a local hospital. The hours worked well with the family when Rita was in school. Enrique's salary paid the bills, but not anymore.

The natural fit would be for Enrique to pursue a degree in the medical field. He wishes he could find something that fit his interests of owning his own restaurant. Food has always been the main focus at all family events. He enjoys making meals for his children from his childhood. Carrying on the ethnic traditions of his family is important to him. It is risky to start your own restaurant. Many fail in the first year. He ponders whether he should look into business or a culinary degree. Which would be more helpful? Then again, he already has a job in the health field and could advance quickly with a four year degree. . . .

Additional Resources to Further Explore Your Major and Career Options

Focus Career and Education Planning System—A free, convenient, online system to further assist CSU students in identifying their personality types and career interests. After completing guided self-assessments students will be able to explore majors and possible career options.

Contact your Introduction to University Life Instructor or the Exploratory Advising Office at *216-687-9376* or email *exploratory.advising@csuohio.edu.*

See *Appendix B* to learn about ways to explore possible majors and careers using Focus 2.

Career Services Center—A place to further explore career options related to majors offered at Cleveland State University. Visit here to look into internships, co-op opportunities, campus employment, and to discuss career opportunities after graduation.

Contact your career coordinator at *careers@csuohio.edu* or visit the CSU Career Services Center website at *http://www.csuohio.edu/offices/career/.*

O*NET Online—Database and interactive application to explore different occupations. It is sponsored by the US Department of Labor and a great source for career exploration. O*NET will assist students in self-assessment and exploration of careers through online assessments.

Access O*NET at *http://www.onetcenter.org*

ADVISOR VISIT

Use this handy worksheet to help you plan your next trip to your advisor. Don't forget to take notes while you are there!

BEFORE THE VISIT

Advisor Name: ____

Advisor Email: _____________________________ Phone:______________________

Date of visit: __________________ Time of visit: ________________

Location: _________________________

Reason for visit: (check all that apply)

- ☐ Discuss my major/change of major
- ☐ Plan courses for next semester
- ☐ To discuss a problem or concern
- ☐ To plan for graduation
- ☐ To discuss course requirements/goals/grades
- ☐ Other:___________________________________

What questions will you ask during the visit?

1. ____

2. ____

3. ____

4. ____

DURING THE VISIT

While meeting with your advisor, take notes on the **back** of this worksheet. Be sure to write the answers to your questions.

Answers to my questions:

Advisor advice:

Things to do:

1. ____________________

2. ____________________

3. ____________________

Schedule your next visit...

Date of next visit:____________________

Time of next visit:____________________

ADVISING VERIFICATION

Advisor Name: ____________________ College: ____________________

Advisor Signature: ____________________ Date: ____________________

Discussion

I am taking a lot of general education requirements. How do I know if they apply to my major?

– Matt

My Mom really wants me to be a nurse, but I hate biology. What should I do?

– Shaunte

It is my senior year and I am seriously considering changing my major. Am I crazy?

– Sean

CHAPTER SEVEN:

THIS IS ONLY A TEST

Exam Preparation and Anxiety Management

"Education is not the learning of facts, but the training of the mind to think."
–Albert Einstein

Sure, you would rather do anything than take an exam. You may doubt your knowledge or study skills. Perhaps you have struggled with test taking in the past. With the following tips for **before, during, and after the exam**, you can develop a plan for success! Which tips have you tried? *Which new tips will you try?*

Before the Test

- Schedule your study sessions well in advance. Begin to study *at least* two weeks prior to each exam. It is important to avoid cramming. Cramming leads to anxiety which may hinder your test performance.
- Be sure you know exactly *when* the test will be, what *format* it will be (multiple choice, essay, fill in), what *chapters* the test will cover, as well as how long you have to take it.
- Come prepared. Do you have the materials you need?
- Eat a nutritious breakfast and arrive early to the exam.
- Wear a watch to monitor your progress.
- Have a POSITIVE ATTITUDE! If you go in telling yourself, "*I am going to fail this*" you will not do so hot. Repeat to yourself an affirmation such as "*I am prepared and ready to do my best!*"

During the Test

- Read the directions very carefully!
- Make the test your own! Skim the entire test and start with a question you are comfortable with.
- Use the process of elimination. Ask if you are allowed to write on the test. Look for the wrong answers first and cross them out. Narrow down your choices.
- Do a "brain dump"; once you get your exam, jot down any formulas or terms you are trying to remember.
- Try covering up the answers. Read the question, determine the answer, and then select the answer that best fits your understanding.
- If you are unsure about a question, be sure to ask the professor.
- Take your time. Remember that test taking is NOT a race!

After the Test

- Check your work prior to turning in the test.
- Once returned, file it away with the notes from that test. You may need to refer to these items in the future, especially if the exam is cumulative.
- Talk with your professor about any questions or concerns you may have.
- Learn from your mistakes and missed questions. Try to avoid making similar mistakes on the next exam.
- Begin to study and create study guides for the next exam.
- Reward yourself for a job well done (if it *was* a job well done, that is). Cupcakes usually do the trick.

Test Anxiety

A certain amount of anxiety before a test is OK—in fact, it can be beneficial and give you that jolt of adrenaline to help you perform better on the exam. But like anything else, too much of a good thing is too much! Too much anxiety can create physical and mental problems, which will hurt your chances of doing well on the exam. In addition, eating right, sleeping right, getting some exercise, scheduling study time and taking breaks after 20–30 minutes of study will go a long way to reduce stress and increase your performance on exams. If you find your anxiety increasing, talk with someone. Sometimes the right person can help us clarify our thoughts and clear up some misconceptions about exams!

Here are some quick suggestions to help battle test anxiety:

- Breathe deeply. Take three long, calming breaths in through your nose and out through your mouth.
- Develop and recite a positive affirmation for test taking. This will help you keep the test in perspective.
- In the restroom or some other private space, shake out your arms and legs. This looks a little funny but it works!
- Listen to relaxing music or a song that makes you feel confident and ready to take control, such as "Eye of the Tiger" by Survivor.

Stress Management

Ahhhhhh!!!!! My life is falling apart! My life is falling apart!

By: Erin Hanrahan, English 101 SLA Leader and CSU student

Stop! Right there. Stop. Inhale deeply. Hold it for a minute. Release it. No, I don't hold a Bachelor of Arts in Yoga or Relaxation Techniques. It's an old trick and people have been giving each other that little tidbit of advice for years for a reason.

Also, stop and think. Make a plan for managing your life and follow it through as much as you can. Academia, regardless of where you intend to go with it—be it a Bachelors degree, then a career, or a Masters degree, then a career—can be all consuming. Manage your academic life appropriately to maximize your chances of success, but also make a healthy amount of time for those aspects outside of your academic life.

1. Take care of yourself. Basically, eat food, and preferably not a double quarter pounder with cheese from McDonald's on a daily basis. No, I'm not telling you to adopt a vegetarian diet and give up root beer. Just make sure you shove fruits and vegetables in there between the root beer and chicken wings.

2. Sleep. Despite what anybody tells you, sleep is not illegal in college or higher education. In fact, if you want to survive college and not end up in the hospital for sleep deprivation (it can happen), you'll make time.

3. Relationships. Make time for family, friends, and significant others. Without them, you'll start talking to yourself in the library study carrels.
4. Socialize. Join clubs. Attend CSU events. You may even win a cool prize for attending!
5. Exercise! Yoga class or a simple 15 minute walk will help you clear your mind and regain focus.

Positive Thinking

"Whether you think you can, or you think you can't–you're right."

The quote above is from Henry Ford. It summarizes a very important message we have for you. **You create your reality.** Seriously. you make your own choices. You can choose to fail or you can choose to succeed. You can choose to study actively or you can choose to update your Facebook status. You can choose to read in the library or you can choose to read in bed. You can choose to go to class or you can choose to sleep in. You can choose to think you can or you can choose to think you can't. You get the point.

Consider this thought:

"I am no good at math. I am not cut out for this statistics class. Hopefully I at least get a C to pass."

How do you think this person will do in the course? Now consider a different thought:

"I am ready to start anew with this math class. I will keep up, seek out the help I need, and do my very best."

How do you think this student will do in the course?

The first thought sets the student up for failure and the student set the bar quite low. The second person acknowledges the past, yet has a positive outlook on what is to come in the class. Remember that your thoughts influence your attitude and outlook. And when you go into class or sit down to study with a good attitude, the experience is more enjoyable. When you enjoy what you are doing, you don't mind doing it. Now don't you want to get to the point where you enjoy studying? It is possible and it starts with your thoughts.

Once you consciously think you will succeed, set your goals (see Chapter One, Go For It!), and think and act like a student ready to learn. But what about those self-doubts? Maybe you never were that great in school, or maybe you are just too hard on yourself. You can change the way you think about yourself. It takes a little practice, self-awareness and dedication. ***Here are some pointers on how to change from negative thinking to positive thinking.***

- This takes practice. Start slowly. It may even help you to write down the self-defeating thoughts to gain awareness.
- Whenever you think a negative thought about yourself (your skills, progress, even appearance) immediately think of a stop sign. Stop the thought and REPLACE it with a positive thought immediately.
- Pay attention to what you verbalize about yourself as well.

Try It! How about for the next exam, you pay conscious attention to what you are telling yourself while in class, while studying and while taking the exam? Be sure to replace the negative thoughts with positive thoughts.

Discussion: Test Taking

Whenever it is a test day, I enter the class feeling confident. However, all of my classmates are frantically comparing notes and asking about terms I did not study. It really freaks me out and I lose all of my confidence. Is there any avoiding this?

– Sheila

Sometimes when I get the test in my hand, I get a little dizzy and tend to "blank out." I feel like I forgot everything I studied the night before. What am I doing wrong?

– Ricky

A few friends of mine share answers from the exam in a number of ways that I am not comfortable disclosing. They try to include me in their "answer ring" but I am hesitant. Is it worth the risk?

– Tony

CAMPUS PROGRAMS AND SERVICES

Campus 411 – All-in-1 Enrollment Services

MC 116

P: (216) 687-5411

http://www.csuohio.edu/enrollmentservices/all-in-1/

© RetroClipArt, 2012. Used under license from Shutterstock, Inc.

Campus Safety/University Police

Campus Safety Building

P: (216) 687-2020 (Escort Service and non emergency number)

Police Emergency number 911 on campus

Email: police@csuohio.edu

http://www.csuohio.edu/offices/police/

Career Services Center

RW 280

P: (216) 687-2233

http://www.csuohio.edu/offices/career/

Child Development Center

Rec. Center

P: (216) 802-3330

http://www.csuohio.edu/services/childcare/

Counseling Center

UN 220

P: (216) 687-2277

http://www.csuohio.edu/offices/counselingcenter/

Disability Services

MC 147

P: (216) 687-2015

http://www.csuohio.edu/offices/disability/

Exploratory Advising/TRIO

MC 110

P: (216) 687-9376

http://www.csuohio.edu/academic/advising/

Health and Wellness Services

UN 263

P: (216) 687-3649

http://www.csuohio.edu/offices/health/

Math Learning Center

MC 230

P: (216) 687-4543

http://www.csuohio.edu/sciences/dept/mathematics/learning_center.html

Office of Diversity and Multicultural Affairs

RT 1254

P: (216) 687-9394

http://www.csuohio.edu/offices/odama/

Student Life

SC 319

P: (216) 687-2048

http://www.csuohio.edu/studentlife/index.html

Testing Center

RTW 215

P: (216) 687-2566

http://www.csuohio.edu/offices/testingcenter/

The Tutoring & Academic Success Center (TASC)

MC 233

P: (216) 687-2012

tutoring@csuohio.edu

http://www.csuohio.edu/academic/advising/tutoring/

- One to One Tutoring
- Success Coaching
- eTutoring
- Supplemental Instruction (SI)
- Structured Learning Assistance (SLA)
- Walk-in Tutoring
- Viking Academic Boot Camp

Veterans Student Success Program

RTW 214

P: (216) 875-9996

http://www.csuohio.edu/studentlife/vikingvets'academic.html

Women's Center

MC 142

P: (216) 687-4674

http://www.csuohio.edu/studentlife/womenscenter/

Writing Center

RT 124

P: (216) 687-6981, x6982

http://www.csuohio.edu/academic/writingcenter/

Helpful Websites

Goal Setting

www.futureme.org

Send a letter to yourself in the future! Future Me is a fun program that allows you to set goals and then check your progress after a defined amount of time.

http://www.cmu.edu/acadev/fastfact/Academic%20Goals08.pdf

"I am going to get a 4.0 this semester by studying every night until 2 a.m. and then getting up at 7 a.m. for my 8 a.m. class." Good luck with that. You should check out this printable PDF providing fast facts on goal setting and the steps required for setting and reaching your academic goals.

Motivation

http://www.studygs.net/motivation/

"The only thing I enjoy more than sleeping in is my late afternoon nap. I love college!" At that rate you would love college for a semester until you are placed on academic probation. Try the activity on this site. Then, you will be able to love college for more than one semester.

Learning Styles

www.vark-learn.com/english/index.asp

Take the VARK test of 13 questions that will help you learn new information. Are you a visual, aural, read/write, kinesthetic learner, or a combination? This site even offers strategies to maximize strengths in real-life learning situations.

http://www.learning-styles-online.com/

This website is dedicated to helping you better understand learning styles, as well as providing an easy way to discover your own styles. "I reviewed my notes for three hours and still failed the test!" Turn your studying from quantity into quality.

Time Management

http://www.studygs.net/shared/mgmnt.htm

"If I took away family, friends, work, sleep, and everything else in my life, then college would be pretty easy." This website offers an extensive guide to develop time management skills. The goal is to succeed in your studies while balancing the demands of family, friends, work, etc.

Studying

http://www.cse.buffalo.edu/~rapaport/howtostudy.html#claxton

Studying can be tiring. Talking about how to study? You might as well press the snooze bar one more time. This website is an entertaining guide on how to study efficiently. The author provides almost forty comic strips on topics such as time management, note taking, homework, test taking, and essay writing.

Note Taking

http://www.dartmouth.edu/~acskills/success/notes.html

Effective note taking continues long after the lecture is over! Dartmouth College provides handouts and videos on how to recall more information from your lectures through active listening and purposeful note-taking.

Active Reading

http://www.dartmouth.edu/~acskills/success/reading.html

"Why do I need help with reading? I have been doing it for a while." Dartmouth College is at it again! This site offers insight into active reading strategies and will help you become a more efficient and effective reader.

Managing Stress

http://www.uhs.uga.edu/stress/

Stress grows like a rolling snowball. However, the sun and a bag of salt will not help melt stress away. This University of Georgia website highlights the components of a lifestyle that will help to reduce stress and prevent some of the problems caused by stress.

Resources on Writing

http://owl.english.purdue.edu/owl/

If you are like most students, you get frustrated with MLA. The Online Writing Lab (OWL) at Purdue University provides writing resources and enables anyone at any time to find answers to questions about writing and improve specific writing skills

Class Presentations

www.prezi.com

Prezi combines concept maps, posters, and presentations all into one very nicely integrated unit. It allows you to create non-linear presentations (so long slide show) where you can zoom in and out of a visual map. The future is now!

Help Wanted

www.khanacademy.org

Need help with mitosis at three in the morning? This website supplies a free online collection of more than 3200 micro lectures via video tutorials stored on YouTube.

GPA Calculator

www.back2college.com/gpa.htm

Calculate your semester and cumulative GPA. Also, determine how many credit hours and what grade average you will need to raise your current GPA.

APPENDIX A

Warning! Before you turn in your paper . . .

Did you use another person's idea, opinion, or theory? If you did you have to be 100% certain that you gave proper credit to the person who thought of it first. If you didn't, this is called plagiarism. If you copied and pasted information from another source in your paper, this is plagiarism. If you paraphrase material but did not cite it, well this is plagiarism too. If you . . . enough of the blame game. Although plagiarism is a serious offense, it is most often unintentional. Here are some tips to remember to avoid plagiarism:

- A Fresh Start: Sandwiches aren't the only thing better fresh! Beginning a paper may be a challenge even for professional writers. It may help to have a fresh perspective. To do this you may want to write a pre-paper. Do not confuse this with additional work; this is time for you to vent, pour all of your ideas onto paper, get rid of negative self-condemnation, and write exactly as you speak. Think of this as the literary equivalent to a giant stress IsoFlex™ ball (or smashing dinner plates).
- Engaged Learning: Have you ever noticed you are more apt to complete an assignment when the subject is more interesting to you? If you have, this means you are more intrinsically motivated to do it because it pertains to your interests and who you are as an individual. Individuality is so important to remember in life and in writing. Don't waste your time trying to sound like someone else! To peak your inspiration, try speaking with your professor to spur some creativity or test out a different approach to your writing topic. Engage yourself with an early working draft that you can write, cut, eliminate, add, draw stick figures . . . whatever you need!
- I Knew That: Before you begin to cite every piece of information in your paper, differentiate between what is known as "common knowledge" or facts that are widely known. For example, it is common knowledge that the Great Lakes are the site of many shipwrecks. An example of knowledge that is not common is in October of 2004 a broken wood ship was found off the shores of Cleveland right near Cleveland State University. It was called the "CSU Wreck" because of its location (CLUE 2005-05-22). Information like this is not commonly known and needs to be documented.
- Quotations: Use them when you take anything directly from a source!
- Paraphrasing: Remember that you still need to cite what you paraphrase and be sure to compare your writing with the original to double check that you used your own words.

APPENDIX B

Focus Career and Education Planning System

By: Andrea Clos, CSU Student and English SLA Leader

Is it a coincidence that "college" and "career" both begin with a 'C'? These probably mean nothing semantically but give it a little thought; there is a definite relationship between the meanings of these two words. What do they mean to you? Whether you imagine a vivid picture spanning from applications and syllabi to stethoscopes and x-ray machines, you probably have some snapshot of how you want your life to look like in ten years. As people, we tend to use a lot of 'when' statements. For example, "when I graduate" or "when I become." This is natural and unique to the human species. Within everyone is the undeniable yearning for a purpose. Thankfully we can move more to the practical rather than the hypothetical to answer an important question: Where do I start?

Faster than you could finish that last sentence, Focus Career and Education Planning will offer personalized support and insight into the world of career readiness by providing meaningful self-assessments, an organized guide for exploring possibilities, and a ready-to-use online career portfolio (yes, your very own)!

The avenue to get to Focus is quite convenient. Simply type in "career focus" in the search bar on CSU's homepage. The next page will be titled by Focus 2's formal name: Focus Career and Educational Planning System. You will see Focus's full name again underlined and in green. Click on it to continue! The next step between you and accessing this "free, convenient, on-line Focus System to begin developing your major and career exploration plan" is creating a new user account by clicking on the Get Started button. Your entire career and education planning tool is waiting for you to begin! Accessing your portfolio does require you to create a username and a password. When I created my account, I used my first name as the username. The database would not accept this. Apparently there is more than one 'Andrea' who is wisely using Focus 2. Who knew? Instead, it suggested that I use my email as my username—this program is so darn smart! Once you are finished securing your account, you will find yourself at Focus 2's Main Menu.

Your Focus 2 account will be divided into five sections. The first is entitled Career Readiness and provides a platform upon which you can organize the details regarding your career and educational goals, your academic strengths, your work experiences and accomplishments, your career planning status, and your personal developmental needs. Whether you are moderately interested in career exploration or not, Focus 2 will suggest the smart steps to take in the right direction to start thinking about your career!

Focus 2 emphasizes learning about . . . yourself! This may sound strange, but completing self-assessments allows for professional reflection. A series of assessments under the *Learn Something About Yourself* category are provided and range from a work interest assessment, a values assessment, to even a leisure interest assessment. If you think that sounds clever, hear this: you may combine any of the multiple assessments to specifically search for occupations! Simply click on *See Your Top Career Choices* to narrow your results!

Do you ever wonder if your major will really lead you to the dream job? How will your classes transform your career plan? Exploring the possibilities is essential for everyone, even if you had your heart set on being a botanist from age three. Focus 2 allows you to research any single occupation by name. You may do an organized search by industry, find out what you can do with your major, explore any occupation associated with any major area of study, and even compare two occupations side by side!

While you are busy exploring careers and majors, be aware of the saving options offered so you don't have to recreate your profile every time you log in. To find out more information about a job or major, click on one. Focus 2 will lead you to an overview page where you may use the side menu to navigate detailed information, ranging from earnings to working conditions for that particular major or career. Below the menu, there is an option to save the career. This will automatically lead you to a page where you reflect on why the occupation appealed to you. Simply click on 'save occupation' and all of this information will now be in your profile. To access your career portfolio, check out the fourth step of *Tying it all Together*. You should see your personalized profile that you may review or print any time, any place.

Next, connect yourself with resources! Explore the recommended tools and websites for Job Boards and internship opportunities. The Focus 2 Job Board Network will link you to National Job Boards, State and Local Job Boards, Military Job Boards, Federal and Local Government Job Boards, Job Boards by Industry Type, Internships (summer, part time, etc.), and Specialty Career Fields.